It's Game Time!

Also by Nicholas J. Rinaldi

The Math Teacher's Toolbox: How to Teach Math to Teenagers and Survive

Communication and Creativity in the Math Classroom: Non-Traditional Activities and Strategies That Stress Life Skills

It's Game Time!

Games to Enhance
Classroom Learning

Nicholas J. Rinaldi

ROWMAN & LITTLEFIELD
Lanham • Boulder • New York • London

Published by Rowman & Littlefield
A wholly owned subsidiary of The Rowman & Littlefield Publishing Group, Inc.
4501 Forbes Boulevard, Suite 200, Lanham, Maryland 20706
www.rowman.com

Unit A, Whitacre Mews, 26-34 Stannery Street, London SE11 4AB

British Library Cataloguing in Publication Information Available

Library of Congress Cataloging-in-Publication Data
Rinaldi, Nicholas J., 1945- author.
  It's game time! : games to enhance classroom learning / Nicholas J. Rinaldi.
    pages cm
  ISBN 978-1-4758-1522-1 (hardcover) — ISBN 978-1-4758-1523-8 (paperback) —
ISBN 978-1-4758-1524-5 (e-book)
  1. Activity programs in education. 2. Educational games. I. Title.
  LB1027.25.R56 2015
  371.3—dc23
                                    2014047248

Printed in the United States of America

Contents

Preface

As a teacher, I have always attempted to keep my students actively involved. One way to accomplish this is through classroom games, which I played often in all my classes.

Throughout my career, I served on a variety of system-wide committees that addressed such topics as curriculum, academic standards, differentiated instruction, leadership, and so on. While working on these committees I had the opportunity to discuss strategies, ideas, and activities with elementary and middle school educators. Several of the games in this book were shared with me by those teachers.

Playing games in the classroom can

- enhance learning by providing a non-tedious form of drill and practice on various topics and skills
- help the students to learn the course content
- make drill and practice pleasant and successful
- offer a change of pace for both the students and the teacher
- be useful in providing for individual differences
- motivate students to improve study habits
- cultivate more desirable attitudes toward the subject matter
- relate course content to individual interests
- be used to introduce new concepts and ideas
- give more students a chance to be successful
- encourage cooperation among students
- help promote student leadership
- be a lot of fun for both the students and the teacher

A student survey (done in math classes) pertaining to classroom competitions seems to indicate that the students derive many benefits from classroom competitions.

Students were asked to respond to each of the following statements using the following codes: SA (Strongly Agree), MA (Mostly Agree), MD (Mostly Disagree), or SD (Strongly Disagree). The results (223 responses) are given below.

The various classroom competitions have . . .

1. helped to improve my math skills. SA (35 percent), MA (57 percent) = 92 percent. MD (7 percent), SD (1 percent) = 8 percent.
2. improved my attitude toward math. SA (22 percent), MA (59 percent) = 81 percent. MD (17 percent), SD (2 percent) = 19 percent.
3. motivated me to improve my study skills. SA (15 percent), MA (55 percent) = 70 percent. MD (24 percent), SD (5 percent) = 29 percent.
4. improved my ability to cooperate with others. SA (30 percent), MA (57 percent) = 87 percent. MD (10 percent), SD (3 percent) = 13 percent.

There are over forty games presented in this book. Many of them were originally used in my math classes; however, by making some adjustments, the vast majority of these games can be used in any class at any level. You must decide when and how to use these games to effectively complement your teaching philosophy and style and to meet the needs of your students.

Many of the games were intended to be played by small groups of students. If you routinely use cooperative learning groups, they can be the teams used in the many competitions in this book. Teams can be formed only for the purposes of playing some of the games. If you wish to form cooperative learning groups, a procedure is suggested below:

*   Based on the students' previous level of achievement (or simply by using your own judgment), arrange them into academically balanced groups of three to five members; that is, each group should have about the same number of strong, average, and below-average students.
*   Select one strong student from each team to serve as the taskmaster or game captain.
*   Another possibility is to simply organize the students into teams randomly. (Fairness of teams is an issue if you use this procedure.)

For details on implementing cooperative learning groups to be used on a regular basis, refer to my first book, *The Math Teacher's Toolbox: How to Teach Math to Teenagers and Survive.* Chapter 4, "And the Children Shall Lead," contains a detailed procedure on how to organize groups and apply group learning. Included are the results of student surveys on the effectiveness of cooperative learning. The appendix of the book contains easily reproducible materials to help implement the process. Included are a team profile, which the students fill out to learn more about each other; several group processing forms, which help students evaluate the effectiveness of their group work; taskmaster duties; taskmaster evaluation forms; and everything you need to conduct a more student-centered classroom.

Introduction

The games in this book are organized by category (although some of the categories do overlap). Next to the title of each game you will see one or more of the following letters: *E, M, H*. These letters indicate that the game is intended primarily for students in elementary, middle, or high school, respectively. However, this is only a guide. There is only one person who knows whether your students will benefit from a particular game, and that is you. You know your students' abilities, their interests, and the types of teaching strategies and activities to which they respond. With some games you may not be sure how your students will react.

Consequently, choose a game and try it with one class. Tell them that after the game has been played, you would appreciate their input and honest constructive criticism. You may find that playing a game exactly the way it is presented in this book may not work for you; therefore you may want to make adjustments to fit your personality and teaching style and the needs of your students. Also, keep in mind that what works with one group of students may not work well with another group. Successful teaching requires periodic analyzing and adjusting.

One of the great things about teaching is that if you try something and it doesn't go smoothly, you can analyze what happened, make the necessary adjustments, and try it again tomorrow, next week, next month, or next year.

Chapter 1 deals with motion/action games. They add an element of mobility and active engagement, which the students, especially the younger ones, seem to enjoy. Some of these games have been successfully used with high school freshmen.

The games in chapter 2 have a sports theme (baseball, football, volleyball, basketball, and hockey/soccer). It is suggested that you organize your class into two teams to play these games. Students also seem more receptive to these games during the appropriate season.

As implied by the title of chapter 3, *Quickies*, these games do not take prior preparation and can be done virtually any time in the class period. Whenever you feel that the class is dragging and you want to raise the energy level, consider playing one of these games.

The games in chapter 4, *Who, What, Where, When?*, do require time to prepare suitable questions for each of the four *W*'s (many suggested questions are included). These games are more challenging and test the knowledge of the students in an out-of-the-ordinary way.

The overwhelming majority of students like to watch television. Chapter 5's games are based on some popular TV game shows, and as such, the students really seem to enjoy playing them.

The games in chapter 6 require significant preparation time. However, once the work has been done, you have these materials to use over and over again. These games are more sophisticated than most of the other games in this book, and the students seem to derive many benefits from playing them. Consequently, they are worth the effort.

Chapter 7 contains a wide variety of games that don't fit into any particular category (or perhaps they fit into many). These games are appropriate for various classes at many levels.

Chapter 8 contains a procedure you can follow that allows your students to create their own games. Also included is a way to enhance holiday fun.

The appendix contains materials that supplement some of the topics presented. These items and many discussed in the book are easily reproducible and ready to use, and as such should help you to save time.

RANDOM STUDENTS

When playing certain games, it may not be possible to call on every student. Tell the students that in order to make the selection process fair, you are going to *randomly* call on them. Here are two ways to do that.

1. You can simply write the name of each student on a small piece of paper (or have the students write them) and place the pieces in a bag. Shake the bag and then draw a name.
2. If you have access to a graphing calculator, use its random number feature:

   ◊ Assign to each student a number from 1 to however many students are in the class. If you use a grade book, use the number next to the student's name in the listing.

◊ On the graphing calculator (a TI-84 Plus in this case) select the MATH key, then PRB, then randInt(. In parentheses enter the number 1 then a comma, followed by the number of students in the class; let's say 25. The display would look like this:

randInt(1, 25)

Hit Enter and a random number from 1 to 25 will appear. Each time you hit Enter, another random number will appear.

Explain to the students that this is equivalent to putting the name of each student on a slip of paper and placing all the slips in a bag, shaking the bag, and drawing a name.

By following either of the above procedures, you usually will not hear comments like "That's not fair, I never got called on." Names are chosen at random; consequently, each student has an equal chance of being selected.

Chapter One

Motion/Action Games

These games are primarily used for drill and practice. They add an element of mobility and active engagement, which the students, especially the younger ones, seem to enjoy. Questions can be from topics you are currently studying or reviewing.

Questions used will vary depending on the subject and the level of the class.

- Math questions might include simple arithmetic problems or exercises from elementary algebra or geometry. Examples: calculate $23 \times 78 \div 39$; what is x if $4x + 7 = 55$; what is the area of a triangle with a base of 12 inches and a height of 8 inches?
- Science questions could be about famous scientists, basic scientific principles, important discoveries, and so on. Examples: Who invented the light bulb? What is the scientific principle that explains why an apple falls off a tree? Who discovered penicillin? The Moon revolves around the Earth in _____ days.
- Social studies questions could address famous historical characters, important dates, significant events, and so on. Examples: Which president abolished slavery? In what year did World War II end? What happened in 1929 that ended an economic boom in America? During the Civil War the capital of the Confederacy was _____.
- Questions from language arts might include vocabulary, grammar, famous authors, and the like. What is the definition of "inundate"? In the sentence "Justin is very happy." what part of speech is the word "very"? Who wrote "The Adventures of Tom Sawyer"?

AROUND THE ROOM (E, M)

Materials needed: flash cards with questions on the topic you are currently covering or wish to review.

Procedure:

- Tell the students to stand.
- The first student in the first row stands next to the second student in the first row.
- Show those two students a flash card. The first one to give the correct answer moves next to the third student in the first row.
- Another flash card is displayed and the winner keeps advancing up and down the rows.
- Students earn one point each time they advance.
- The student who earns the most points is the winner.
- Note: although only two students are actively participating at any given time, the teacher should encourage the other students to play along to see if they can come up with the correct answer before either of the contestants; the idea is to keep as many students as possible actively involved.

STATION TO STATION (E, M, H)

Materials needed: Numbered 5" × 7" index cards (or half sheets of paper) containing questions, one per card. One sheet of paper per student, numbered from 1 to as many questions as you are using. Allow enough space in each numbered area for both the question and answer.

Procedure:

- Place one card on each desk in the room.
- Tell the students that at your signal they are to copy the question in front of them onto the paper provided, and then put the answer below it.
- After you say "Begin," each student works on the question.
- After a sufficient amount of time, instruct students to *change stations*—that is, to move to another desk, according to a plan students were given prior to the beginning of the game. (It's probably a good idea to display a diagram of the plan on the board.)
- While at the new desk, again students are to copy the question and put the answer in the appropriate place.

- This process continues until each student has answered every question.
- At that point, go over the answers and address any questions that caused trouble.

This game works especially well with younger students, but older students seem to enjoy it also.

LOG JAM (E, M, H)

Materials needed: As with Station to Station, give each student a piece of paper numbered from 1 to as many questions as you are using. Allow enough space in each numbered area for both the question and answer.

Procedure:

- Again have questions (similar to those for Station to Station) for the students to work on written on 5" × 7" file cards, one at each desk.
- This time, however, after the student has answered the question, he/she immediately passes it on to another student according to a plan explained to them prior to the game. (Again, it is probably a good idea to display a diagram of the plan on the board.)
- As might be expected, the slower-working students do not pass on the questions as quickly as most, hence the name *Log Jam.*
- It is wise to have some extra questions, perhaps of a more challenging nature, on the board for those who have a long wait between turns.
- After all the students have answered all the questions, go over the answers and provide help with those questions that caused trouble.

CATCH! (E, M)

Objective: to give the students drill and practice in a fun way.
Materials needed: a Nerf ball, rolled up sock, or something similar to be used as a ball.

Procedure:

- The teacher begins by tossing a small soft ball to a student and then asks a question from the current lesson or a review lesson.

- If the student gets it wrong, he/she must toss the ball back to the teacher who in turn tosses it to another student.
- If the question is correctly answered, then the student can toss the ball to a classmate who then gets the next question.
- Play continues as described above.

Students really enjoy this game for two reasons: (1) they like to throw things and (2) they like the control of tossing the ball to a friend of their choosing.

LAST MAN STANDING (E, M)

Objective: to give the students drill and practice or to go over homework.

Procedure:

- To begin, the students are to complete a set of exercises from the textbook or a worksheet.
- All the students now stand up next to their desks.
- The teacher now gives the answers to the exercises, one at a time.
- If the student gets an answer wrong, he/she sits down.
- Continue through the rest of the answers.
- The last one(s) standing win the game (and perhaps a predetermined reward).

YES, YOU CAN! (E, M)

Objective: to give the students drill and practice or to go over homework.
Materials needed: a Nerf ball, rolled up sock, or something similar to be used as a ball

Procedure:

- This is a team game where the rows of students are the teams.
- The teacher calls a row to the front of the room.
- The first student is asked a question from the current unit of work, from the previous homework assignment, or from review material.
- If the student gets it right, one point is earned for his/her team.

- The student then gets to toss a ball at the trash can. If the student makes the basket, one additional point is added to the team score.
- If the student gets the answer wrong, no point is awarded and the student is not given the chance to throw for an additional point.
- It is now the turn of the next person in that team.
- Play continues as described above until each member of each team has had a turn.
- The team with the highest score wins.

ONE-ON-ONE (E, M)

Objective: to give the students drill and practice.

Procedure:

- Divide the class into two teams.
- The first student from each team comes to the board and picks up a marker.
- The teacher reads a problem or question to the students (this game works especially well with simple math problems).
- The first student to write the correct answer on the board wins a point for his/her team.
- Now call up the next two players. Play continues until each player on each team has had a turn.

Chapter Two

Sports Games

These classroom games simulate playing popular sports in our society: baseball, football, volleyball, basketball, soccer, and hockey. Many students strongly identify with them because they actually play these sports in real life or follow their favorite college or professional team(s) on TV or in person. Consequently, students are usually enthusiastic participants when these games are played in the classroom.

These games can be used primarily for drill and practice, or to go over homework. (If students know beforehand that they will be called on for answers, which can affect the outcome of a game, they are more likely to do the homework).

CLASSROOM BASEBALL (M, H)

Students are usually most receptive to this game at the beginning of baseball season (April) and especially around World Series time (October).

Materials needed:

• You will need a drawing or representation of *a baseball field* to be displayed so that all can see it.
  ◊ If you place the field on a flat surface, pennies, chips, or similar objects can be used to represent base runners. If you use an overhead projector, make a transparency of the baseball field. (Images of baseball fields can be found at Google Images/baseball fields.) The photograph/drawing of the field can also be attached to a bulletin board, and the base runners can be represented by small squares of paper, which can be attached by thumb tacks.

◊ A piece of pegboard with a baseball field drawn on it or a picture of one taped to it can also be used. There should be holes at the locations representing each base. Golf tees can be used to represent the players on base by inserting the tee into the hole.

- You will also need several *questions/problems* pertaining to the topic you wish to work on. These questions/problems can be taken out of the book, from a worksheet, displayed on the overhead projector or computer, etc.

Procedure

- Divide the room into two teams and decide which team bats first. If the game is played during World Series time, the two teams can represent those in the World Series.
- Each team is to determine a batting order; this can be done by an elected (or appointed) team captain, or by the teacher.
- The first member of the team at bat goes head-to-head with the first member of the team on the field. The first question/problem is now presented on the overhead projector, on the board, on a flash card, or from a book or worksheet. Only these two players are allowed to answer this question and they do so by calling out the answer.
- If the player representing the team at bat (offense) is first to give the correct answer, the batter is awarded a single and a marker is placed on first base. If the answer is incorrect, the player is out. If the player representing the team in the field (defense) is first to give the correct answer, the batter is out. If the answer is incorrect, the batter is awarded a single.
- Now it's the turn of player number two from each team. If the previous batter was correct, and the next batter gives the correct answer before the defensive player, this player is awarded a double; that is, two correct answers in a row result in a double. If three batters in a row answer correctly, the current batter is awarded a triple; for four in a row and each *successive* correct answer thereafter, the batter has hit a homerun. If at any time the defensive player gives the correct answer first, the batter is out and the next correct answer given by the batter results only in a single.
- If there is at least one runner on base, and less than two outs, and the batter answers *incorrectly*, a member of the other team is randomly chosen. If he/she gives the correct answer, a double play has been turned by the defense; in this case the batter and the furthest advanced runner are out. If the defensive player is incorrect, only the previous batter is out. Once three outs have been recorded, the second team has its turn at bat, and play continues as described above.

- At any point during an inning, the captain of the defensive team (the team not batting) may call for a *"relief pitcher."* The relief pitcher is a player on the defensive team that the captain chooses to go head-to-head with the next batter.
  ◊ Both players are given a question simultaneously. Answers are shouted out.
  ◊ If the batter answers correctly first, he/she is awarded the amount of bases associated with the problem.
  ◊ If the batter answers first and is incorrect, he/she is out.
  ◊ If the relief pitcher then gives the correct answer, the result is a double play (see above). If the relief pitcher answers correctly first, the batter is out.
  ◊ A maximum of two relief pitchers may be used in any inning.
  ◊ During the game, any player may be used as a relief pitcher only once.
- The length of the game depends on the time available. You can attempt to play as many complete innings as time allows, or you can play for a specified time.

An alternate approach is to organize the questions into four levels of difficulty: relatively easy questions are worth a single; questions a bit more difficult are worth a double; and so on. When the player comes to bat, he/she chooses whether he/she wants to try for a single, double, triple, or homerun. If answered correctly, the batter is awarded the number of bases associated with that question. The other rules stay the same.

Play ball!

CLASSROOM FOOTBALL (M, H)

Students are usually most receptive to this game during football season (September to January) and especially close to Super Bowl time (late January to early February).

Materials needed:

- You will need a drawing or a representation of *a football field* to be displayed so that all can see it.
  ◊ If you place the field on a flat surface, a coin can be used to represent the position of the ball. If you use an overhead projector, make a transparency of the football field. (Images of football fields can be found at Google Images/football fields).

◊ The photograph/drawing of the field can also be attached to a bulletin board, and the ball can be represented by a small piece of paper, which can be attached by a thumb tack.

◊ A piece of pegboard with a football field drawn on it or a picture of one taped to it can also be used. There should be holes at the locations representing each goal line and yard markers, 10 yards apart. A golf tee can be used to represent the position of the ball by inserting the tee into the holes.

- You will also need several *questions/problems* pertaining to the topic you wish to work on. These questions/problems can be taken out of the book, from a worksheet, displayed on the overhead projector or computer, etc.

Procedure

- Divide the room into two teams. If the game is being played during Super Bowl time, the two teams can represent those that are playing in that year's game.
- A coin toss decides which team goes first.
- Teams have four downs (tries) to advance the ball as far as they can, or to score.
- The team that wins the toss has the ball placed on its own 20-yard line.
- A member of the offensive team is chosen at random and asked a question.
  ◊ If it is correctly answered, the ball is advanced 10 yards. A second member of the offensive team is then chosen and asked another question. If it is correctly answered, the ball is advanced 20 yards; if a third *consecutive* question is correctly answered, the ball is advanced 30 yards, and a fourth *consecutive* correct answer results in another 30 yard gain (and necessarily, a touchdown).
  ◊ If a question is answered incorrectly, a member of the defensive team is randomly chosen and asked the same question. If correctly answered, the ball moves *back* 10 yards; if answered incorrectly, the ball stays where it is. In either case the turn goes back to the offense (unless it was fourth down) to resume answering questions; however the consecutive answer string has been broken, and the question is only worth 10 yards.
- If the ball is advanced to the goal line or beyond, a touchdown is scored.
- A point-after is attempted in the following way:
  ◊ A question is designated for all to attempt; that is, everyone is told, for example, "For the point after, try number 14 on the worksheet. When you think you know the answer, shout it out."
  ◊ If a member of the offensive team answers first and is correct, the point is good; if he/she is incorrect, the point is no good.

◊   If a member of the defensive team answers first and is correct, the point is no good; if he/she is incorrect, the point is good.

• After the point-after attempt, the team that was formally on defense now goes on offense with the ball on their 20-yard line and play proceeds as described above.

• The game is over when a previously specified time is reached.

CLASSROOM VOLLEYBALL (E, M, H)

To set up the game, begin by selecting a system that allows you to randomly choose students:

• Approach 1: Divide the class into two groups of about equal size; let's say rows 1–3 and rows 4–6. Pass out small slips of paper, one to each student. Have the student write his/her name on the paper. Rows 1–3 are Team A and their names go into a small bag labeled "A." Rows 4–6 are Team B and their names go into another small bag labeled "B." To conserve time you can perform this task prior to the class.

• Approach 2: Obtain a graphing calculator. Again those in rows 1–3 are Team A and the students in rows 4–6 are Team B. Assign to each member of Team A a number from 1 to how many are in the team, let's say 1–13. Assign to members of Team B the numbers 14 on until all have a number. To randomly select a student using the calculator, see "Random Students" in the introduction of this book.

Procedure

• Begin by flipping a coin to decide which team "serves" first; let's say it's A. Using either of the above methods, select a student at random from Team A. (If you are using a calculator and a number outside of the range of numbers for those in Team A appears, continue to press Enter until an appropriate number appears.) The student is given a question from the textbook or a worksheet.

• If the student answers correctly, he/she is considered to have hit the ball over the net into Team B's court. Now randomly choose a student from Team B, who is given a question. If he/she answers it correctly, the ball is considered to have been hit back over the net.

• Play continues until one team gets the answer wrong. When that happens, this team has lost the point which is given to the other team. As long as a team wins the point, they continue to serve.

• The game continues until a specified number of points is obtained, or a predetermined time is reached.

CLASSROOM BASKETBALL (E, M, H)

Set up the class as described above in Classroom Volleyball.

Materials needed: several questions organized into three groups according to level of difficulty: (1) easy, (2) moderate, and (3) difficult.

Procedure:

• Begin by flipping a coin to decide which team has the ball first; let's say it's A.
• Randomly choose a member of Team A who must decide whether he/she wishes to attempt a 2- or 3-point shot.
• If the student wishes to attempt a 2-point shot, give that student a question from the moderate category; if the student wishes to attempt a 3-point shot, give that student a question from the difficult category.
• If the question is answered correctly, Team A scores the point value of the question; if the question is correctly answered within five seconds (or another suitable time limit), the player can earn a bonus point (foul shot) by answering a question in the easy (1 point) category.
• If the question is answered incorrectly, randomly choose a member from Team B who is given the *same* question (this increases the chances of Team B members paying attention).
  ◊ If the answer is correct, Team B scores the point value of the question (the 1-point bonus question is not available on a second chance question).
  ◊ If the answer is incorrect, no points are scored on that question.
  ◊ Give the correct answer and randomly choose a member of Team B (since the round started with Team A, it is now Team B's turn).
• Play continues as described above until a predetermined number of points is scored or until the time limit set is up.

CLASSROOM HOCKEY OR SOCCER (E, M, H)

Select a system that allows you to randomly choose students. (See "Volleyball" above.) Divide the room into two teams; call them Team A and Team B.

Procedure

- Begin by flipping a coin to decide which team goes first; let's say it's Team A. Select a student at random from Team A. (If you are using a calculator and a number outside of the range of numbers for those in team A appears, continue to press Enter until an appropriate number appears.) The student is given a question, which can be from the textbook, a worksheet, etc.
- If the student answers correctly, he/she is considered to have taken a shot at the goal. Now randomly choose a student from Team B. who is given a question. If he/she answers it correctly, the shot is considered to have been blocked (saved). Team B now shoots at Team A's goal, and play continues.
- Any time a question is not answered correctly, that team loses their chance to shoot at its opponent's goal and the opponent now becomes the shooting team.
- The game continues until a specified number of points is obtained, or a predetermined time is reached.

Chapter Three

Quickies

These games take little or no preparation. They are especially effective whenever you feel that the class is dragging and you want to raise the energy level.

FINGER MATH (E)

Objective: to give the students practice with number facts.

Procedure

- Begin by having all the students sit on the floor.
- Randomly choose two students to stand and face each other.
- At the count of 3, each student is to put out their hands with fingers extended from each hand.
- A student wins if he/she is the first to correctly state how many fingers the other is holding out.
- The winner remains standing for the next round, while the loser goes to his/her seat.
- Randomly choose another student to face the winner, and play continues until only one student remains.

As an alternative, the students could be required to subtract the smaller number from the larger, or multiply the number of fingers together.

The next three games can be used to go over homework or for drill and practice. If you are choosing the latter, select a list of questions/problems from the textbook, worksheet, etc.

TIC-TAC-TOE (E, M, H)

To begin, put the traditional tic-tac-toe lines on the board. For easier reference, number the cells.

1	2	3
4	5	6
7	8	9

Procedure

- The teams will be the left half of the room, which is Team X, against the right half, which is Team O.
- Ask the first question, either from the homework or another source. Allow a few seconds for all to consider the answer.
- Then flip a coin to decide which team responds first; let's say it's Team X.
- Then call on someone from Team X. If that person gets the correct answer, he/she will tell you into which cell the team letter (X) will be placed. If the person is incorrect, call on someone from Team O. If he/she is correct then he/she can indicate into which cell the team letter will be placed.
- Since the previous round started with Team X, it is now Team O's turn.
- Play continues as described above.
- The first team to get the traditional three in a row wins the game.

This game can also be played with the teacher vs the class. Follow the procedure above, but if the student called on gives an incorrect answer, then you choose the cell in which to enter your symbol. This is a game you hope you lose.

SUPER TIC-TAC-TOE (E, M, H)

This is a variation of the traditional Tic-Tac-Toe game. Begin with the drawing below. Number the cells for convenience.

1	2	3	4
5	6	7	8
9	10	11	12
13	14	15	16

Procedure

Follow the procedure for Tic-Tac-Toe. The winning team is the first to get:

- four of their symbols in a row vertically, horizontally, or diagonally; or
- their symbol in the four corner spaces (1, 4, 13, and 16); or
- four touching spaces which form a square (for example, 2, 3, 6, 7).
- Again, this game can also be played with the teacher against the class.

Students seem to enjoy this game because there is more strategy than the traditional Tic-Tac-Toe and the game is less likely to end in a tie.

As an extension and perhaps an extra project for older, more ambitious students, suggest that they try the game with a 5 × 5 array of 25 cells; or a 6 × 6 array of 36 cells; or an *n* × *n* arrangement. Ask them to decide whether similar rules for a 4 × 4 array are sufficient or if changes need to be made. Ask what else they find different as the number of cells increases. Give them a couple of days to work on this and then have them report back to the class with their findings.

FOUR-IN-A-ROW (E, M, H)

This game is somewhat similar to Tic-Tac-Toe. It also provides students with practice specifying location by identifying row and column.

Procedure

- If possible, project a transparency of a piece of ¼-inch graph paper on the board. Outline a square 10 × 10. As an alternative, simply draw a box, 10 squares by 10 squares on the board.
- Divide the class into two teams, Team X and Team O. Play procedures are as described in Tic-Tac-Toe.
- If the student called on correctly answers the first question, he/she chooses a square into which the team symbol is placed. The location can be given be saying something like "row two column five." Teams alternate turns. The winning team is the one to first get four of their symbols in a row, either vertically, horizontally, or diagonally.

Again, this game can also be played with the teacher against the class.

THE WEAKEST LINK (E, M)

This is a good game to practice spelling. Have a list of vocabulary words available.

Procedure

- Have all your students stand up next to their seats.
- State the first word to be spelled.

- The first person in a randomly chosen row says the first letter of the word; the second person says the second letter; the third person says the third letter, and so on. Continue into the next row if necessary.
- If the word is misspelled, the student who gives the first wrong letter must sit down, and the spelling of the word is continued. Once the word is correctly spelled, a new word is given and play continues with the next person in sequence. The winner is the last student standing.

Chapter Four

Who, What, Where, When?

These games require time to prepare suitable questions for each of the four *W*'s (many sample questions are below). These games are more challenging than most of the games in this book, and they test the knowledge of the students in uncommon ways, which they seem to enjoy.

WHO AM I? (M, H)

This game was conceived as a team activity, but it can be played on an individual basis. The objective is to be the first player or team to analyze a series of clues to determine the identity of a person or thing using a minimum number of clues.

To play:

- To begin, the students move into their regular cooperative learning groups. (If groups are not regularly used, they can be put together for the purposes of this game.)
- Make a transparency of the clues (see below for samples). Put the transparency on the overhead projector, but cover them such that all but the first clue is hidden. (If an overhead projector is not available, the clues could be written on the board). The objective is for the team to guess the solution.
- If a team thinks they have the solution, they say "stop." Then they write the question number and the answer on a small piece of paper, along with their team name and bring the paper to you.
  ◊ If the team is correct, the point value of the clue is awarded and the round is over.

◊ If the team is not correct, they score zero and the team is eliminated from this round of play.
- The game continues; that is, additional clues are revealed, one at a time, until the last clue is given.
- At any point, a team may guess the answer (following the procedure given above) in an attempt to gain the point value of the clue. Obviously, the more clues they see increases their chance of getting the correct answer, but each additional clue given lowers the potential score. (Decisions, decisions!!)
- After the final clue is revealed, the scores for round one are recorded. The running scores should be listed on the board (the score may affect a team's strategy) and the game continues.
- At the end of the game the winning team(s) or individuals are rewarded with extra credit or a treat.

Below are some sample clues that can be used for this game.

Sample Clues for Who Am I?

In a Math Class

(5 points) I am a two-digit number.
(4 points) I am larger than 30 but smaller than 85; that is, $30 < x < 85$.
(3 points) I am a perfect square.
(2 points) The sum of my digits is 9.
(1 point) I am the solution of the equation $2x + 3 = 75$.
(Solution: I am 36.)

(5 points) I am an eight-letter word.
(4 points) I contain two *E*'s and one *O*.
(3 points) I have a powerful personality.
(2 points) I am a superscript.
(1 point) When I am a positive integer, I tell how many times a base is used as a factor.
(Solution: I am an exponent.)

(5 points) I am a three-digit number.
(4 points) All my digits are the same.
(3 points) All my digits are odd.
(2 points) All my digits are prime.
(1 point) The sum of my digits is a perfect square.
(Solution: I am 333.)

In a Science Class

(5 points) I was born in Germany on March 14, 1879.
(4 points) In 1921 I received the Nobel Prize in Physics.
(3 points) In 1933 I settled in the United States and became an American citizen.
(2 points) My identity is relatively easy to figure out.
(1 point) I am best known for my mass-energy equivalence formula: $e = mc^2$.
(Solution: I am Albert Einstein.)

(5 points) I am a well-known British thinker.
(4 points) My main areas of study are biology and medicine.
(3 points) Many people of my time considered my ideas sacrilegious.
(2 points) Some of my most famous theories were conceived on the Galapagos Islands.
(1 point) I believe in natural selection.
(Solution: I am Charles Darwin.)

In an English Class

(5 points) I was born on April 26, 1564, and died on April 23, 1616.
(4 points) I am often called England's national poet.
(3 points) My works include over one hundred fifty sonnets and about forty plays.
(2 points) My plays have been translated into every major living language and are performed more often than any other playwright.
(1 point) I am widely regarded as the greatest writer in the English language.
(Solution: I am William Shakespeare.)

(5 points) I am a fictional character.
(4 points) I am the central figure in a book written by Daniel Defoe in 1719.
(3 points) I was stranded on an island for twenty-eight years.
(2 points) I saved a man from being eaten by cannibals.
(1 point) His name was Friday.
(Solution: I am Robinson Crusoe.)

In a Social Studies Class

(5 points) I was born in 1809.
(4 points) I was self-educated and became a country lawyer.
(3 points) In the 1830s I was a Whig Party leader and an Illinois state legislator.

(2 points) In 1858 I had a series of debates with my archrival, Stephen A. Douglas.

(1 point) I served as president of the United States from March 4, 1861, until I was assassinated on April 15, 1865.

(Solution: I am Abraham Lincoln.)

(5 points) I was born in Atlanta in 1929.

(4 points) I died at the hands of an assassin in 1968.

(3 points) I am a Nobel Prize winner.

(2 points) I was the son of a preacher.

(1 point) I am famous for saying, "I have a dream."

(Solution: I am Martin Luther King, Jr.)

In Any Class

(5 points) I am a fictional character.

(4 points) Books about me are the most popular series of books ever written, having sold over two hundred million in more than two hundred countries.

(3 points) My first movie hit the theaters in 2001.

(2 points) I am British by birth.

(1 point) Look closely and you will see a lightning-shaped scar on my forehead.

(Solution: I am Harry Potter.)

(5 points) I was born in Chicago in 1901 and died in 1966.

(4 points) I have won more Oscar awards than anyone else.

(3 points) I am a famous cartoonist.

(2 points) I am also a renowned film animator.

(1 points) I have theme parks in Hong Kong, France, and the United States.

(Solution: I am Walt Disney.)

It does take time to prepare all the clues, but once that task is done, especially if the questions and answers are classic, you have these clues to use over and over again. After you have played the game, consider having the students put together some clues and solutions as an extra credit project. Doing this is a good learning experience for the students and will save you some time.

WHAT AM I? (M, H)

The rules are the same as those for "Who Am I?"

Sample Clues for "What Am I?"

In a Geometry Class

(5 points) I am an instrument used to make measurements.
(4 points) Part of me is a straight edge.
(3 points) Part of me is curved.
(2 points) I am used to measure angles.
(1 point) When voting on tractors, I vote pro.
(Solution: I am a protractor.)

(5 points) I am a line segment.
(4 points) I can be found in a triangle.
(3 points) When in a triangle, there are three of me.
(2 points) I extend from a vertex to the line containing the opposite side.
(1 point) I form a right angle.
(Solution: I am an altitude.)

(5 points) I am a polygon.
(4 points) My name contains two words.
(3 points) I am formed by three non-collinear segments.
(2 points) Some think I am sharp.
(1 point) All my angles are less than 90 degrees.
(Solution: I am an acute triangle.)

In a Science Class

(5 points) I am a mysterious wonder.
(4 points) Several songs have been written about me.
(3 points) I am very colorful.
(2 points) I am associated with ROY G. BIV.
(1 point) Some say that at the end of me there is a pot of gold.
(Solution: I am a rainbow.)

(5 points) I am utilized for communication.
(4 points) The first one of me was used in 1957.
(3 points) My use ushered in the Space Age.
(2 points) Hundreds of me are now orbiting the earth.

(1 point) Our own moon is a natural one of me.
(Solution: I am a satellite.)

In an English Class

(5 points) I am a kind of book.
(4 points) I am used for reference.
(3 points) I help you to pronounce words.
(2 points) I also help you with spelling.
(1 point) Webster and American Heritage are two of my most common brands.
(Solution: I am a dictionary.)

(5 points) I am a capital letter of the English alphabet.
(4 points) I am not a vowel.
(3 points) I am included in the first thirteen letters.
(2 points) Part of me is curved.
(1 point) Candy canes are basically shaped like me.
(Solution: I am J.)

In a Social Studies Class

(5 points) I am perhaps the most famous document in U.S. history.
(4 points) I was written in the eighteenth century.
(3 points) I have three parts: The preamble; a list of charges against King George III; the conclusion.
(2 points) I was unanimously approved on July 4, 1776.
(1 point) I announced to the world the unanimous decision of the thirteen colonies to separate from Great Britain.
(Solution: I am The Declaration of Independence.)

(5 points) I was approved on September 6, 1787.
(4 points) My current name did not come into general use until the early nineteenth century.
(3 points) I currently have 538 members.
(2 points) My membership in each state is equal to the number of members of Congress to which the state is entitled.
(1 point) I am the organization that officially elects the president and vice president of the United States.
(Solution: I am the Electoral College.)

In Any Class

(5 points) I am an essential commodity.

(4 points) I am the number-one item sold in grocery stores across America. Ninety-seven percent of all shoppers buy me.

(3 points) I am found in the bathroom.

(2 points) Some call me a roll model.

(1 point) If I were in the navy I might be called a rear admiral.

(Solution: I am toilet paper.)

(5 points) I was invented in the year 1913.

(4 points) I am usually made of metal.

(3 points) I am found on clothing.

(2 points) I can be dangerous.

(1 point) I am a type of fastener that sometimes replaces buttons.

(Solution: I am a zipper.)

WHERE AM I? (M, H)

Social Studies and U.S. Geography

This game helps students learn state locations, capitals, cities, and interesting facts about the states. Materials needed: a transparency of a blank map of the United States and a list of questions (samples are given below). To play the game:

- Go to Google and enter *printable blank maps of the United States* in the search box.
- Make a transparency of the map and then number each state from 1 to 50.
- Place the map on the overhead projector. (If you have the appropriate technology, scan the map into the computer and then project it on the white board.)
- Read one of the questions and give the students about ten seconds to think about the answer.
- Randomly call on a student.
- If he/she gives the right answer, write his/her name in the state (or next to it if it is a small state).
- If an incorrect answer is given, randomly call on other students until the question is answered correctly. (You may wish to set a limit of five incorrect responses before giving the correct answer and going on to the next question.)

• The student who has his/her name written in the most states is the winner.

Sample Questions:

1. The Grand Canyon is located in this state. (Arizona)
2. What state on the map is labeled with the number____? (see second bullet on p. 24)
3. The capital of this state is Denver. (Colorado)
4. Mount Rushmore is located in this state. (N. Dakota)
5. This state is home for the Kansas City Royals and the Kansas City Chiefs. (Missouri)
6. Abraham Lincoln, the sixteenth president of the United States, was born in this state. (Kentucky)
7. Austin, Houston, and Dallas are major cities in this state. (Texas)
8. What state on the map is labeled with the number____? (see second bullet on p. 24)
9. The only two states bordering this state are Georgia and Alabama. (Florida)
10. With reference to land areas, the three largest states are Alaska, Texas, and California. Which state is fourth largest? (Montana)
11. Topeka is the capital of this Midwestern state. (Kansas)
12. This is the only New England state that *does not* have a coastline. (Vermont)
13. _____ was the first state to enter the Union (1638) while _____ was the last (1959). (Delaware; Hawaii)
14. What state on the map is labeled with the number____? (see second bullet on p. 24)
15. As of 2010, this state was the most populous state, containing more people than the 21 least populous states combined. (California)
16. The U.S. Military Academy at West Point is in this state. (New York)
17. The Four Corners is a region of the United States consisting of the southwestern corner of Colorado, northwestern corner of New Mexico, northeastern corner of Arizona, and southeastern corner of _____. (Utah)
18. What state on the map is labeled with the number ____? (see second bullet on p. 24)
19. Although it also extends into Montana and Idaho, Yellowstone National Park is located primarily in this state. (Wyoming)
20. Lincoln is the capital of this state. (Nebraska)

Math

Procedure:

- Draw the x- and y-axes on the board.
- Read one of the questions (sample questions are below) and give the students about ten seconds to think about the answer.
- Randomly call on a student.
- If he/she gives the right answer, write his/her name in the quadrant or on the axis.
- If an incorrect answer is given, randomly call on other students until the question is answered correctly. (You may to set a limit of three incorrect answers before going on to the next question.)
- The student who has his/her name written the most times is the winner.

Choices for answers: Q1, Q2, Q3, Q4, x-axis, y-axis. More than one answer is possible.

Sample Questions

1. My coordinates are (3, 7).
2. My coordinates are (–5, –9).
3. My coordinates are (4, –6).
4. My coordinates are (–2, 8).
5. My coordinates are (0, y).
6. My coordinates are both positive.
7. My coordinates are both negative.
8. My coordinates are (x, 0).
9. My coordinates have the same sign.
10. My coordinates have opposite signs.
11. My coordinates are equal.
12. I am the intersection of the lines with equations $y = 2x + 5$ and $y = -3x + 5$.
13. I am a line with equation $x = 7$.
14. I am a line with equation $y = -9$.
15. I am a line with equation $x = -2$.
16. I am a line with equation $y = 4$.
17. My coordinates are (0, 0).
18. I am the intersection of the lines with equations $y = 2$ and $x = -3$.
19. I am the intersection of the lines with equations $y = -5$ and $x = 4$.
20. I am a line with equation $y = x$.

Answers:

1. Q1
2. Q3
3. Q4
4. Q2
5. *y*-axis
6. Q1
7. Q3
8. *x*-axis
9. Q1, Q3
10. Q2, Q4

11. Q1,Q3
12. *y*-axis
13. Q1,Q4
14. Q3,Q4
15. Q2,Q3
16. Q1,Q2
17. *x*-axis, *y*-axis
18. Q2
19. Q4
20. Q1,Q3

Science

Procedure:

- Organize the class into three teams of about the same size.
- Randomly select one student from each team to go to the board.
- Each is to write the words *land*, *sea*, and *air* side by side.
- Read the names of the animals on a list you have compiled (see samples below).
- The students at the board are to place each name under one of the three headings.
- These students then take their seats.
- Randomly choose three different students from each team and send them to the board.
- These students may then make any changes they feel are necessary.
- The team with the most correct answers wins the game.

Sample Questions

Are the following animals land inhabitants, sea creatures, or birds?

1. Kestrel (Bird, kestrels are a kind of falcon.)
2. Tapir (Land, A tapir is a large herbivorous mammal, similar in shape to a pig.)
3. Sloth (Land, sloths are tree-living mammals from South and Central America.)
4. Christmas tree worm (Sea, these worms are anchored in live calcareous coral.)
5. Fathead (Sea, fathead is a species of temperate freshwater fish.)

6. Toucan (Bird, Toucans are brightly colored tropical birds with very large bills.)
7. Tamarin (Land, type of monkey)
8. Komondor (Land, a large, white-colored Hungarian breed of livestock guardian dog)
9. Aye-aye (Land, The aye-aye is a lemur, a primate native to Madagascar.)
10. Trogon (Bird, a tropical bird)

English

Procedure:

- Arrange the class into teams of four or five students. Let's call them Team 1, Team 2, Team 3, and so on. Another possibility is to have the teams choose their own names.
- Give each team five index cards. Each card will have an A, B, C, D, or E printed on it.
- List the team names on the board.
- Announce to the students the name of one of the authors listed. Give them some time to discuss among themselves where that author was born. (See choices on p. 29.)
- Randomly choose one of the teams for an answer; let's say it is Team 3.
- Once Team 3 gives their answer, don't acknowledge whether or not it is correct.
- Now allow any team that wishes to challenge that answer the opportunity to do so. This is done by the team raising one of the index cards indicating which answer they think is correct.
- All challenging teams must raise their cards at the same time.
- If Team 3's answer is correct, they earn one point. Any team that challenged that correct answer loses one point.
- If Team 3 is incorrect, there is no penalty (they were forced to do that problem). Then any team correctly challenging the answer earns one point; incorrect challenges lose one point.
- Turns rotate with the next team in order going next; in this example that would be Team 4.
- Indicate the team score on the board after each round.
- Play continues until all the questions are asked or until time runs out.
- The team with the most points win.

Sample Questions

Where were each of these famous authors born? Choose from (A) United States, (B) United Kingdom, (C) India, (D) Ireland, or (E) Russia

1. Ernest Hemingway (A)
2. Mark Twain (A)
3. William Shakespeare (B)
4. Stephen King (A)
5. Charles Dickens (B)
6. Edgar Allan Poe (A)
7. Leo Tolstoy (E)
8. Lewis Carroll (B)
9. Walt Whitman (A)
10. George Orwell (C)
11. Oscar Wilde (D)
12. F. Scott Fitzgerald (A)
13. James Joyce (D)
14. William Faulkner (A)
15. Virginia Woolf (B)
16. Ralph Waldo Emerson (A)
17. Ray Bradbury (A)
18. Agatha Christie (B)

WHEN AM I? (M, H)

Science

The procedure is the same as the one used above.

Sample Questions

When were each of these famous scientists born? Choose from (A) prior to the first century (B) 1501–1700, (C) 1701–1800, (D) 1801–1900, (E) 1901–2000

1. Albert Einstein (D)
2. Galileo Galilei (B)
3. Marie Curie (D)
4. Louis Pasteur (D)
5. Aristotle (A)

6. Thomas Edison (D)
7. Alexander Graham Bell (D)
8. Gregor Mendel (D)
9. Johannes Kepler (B)

In which of the time periods listed above were each of these scientific discoveries made?

1. Gravity (B)
2. The wheel (A)
3. Theory of Evolution (D)
4. Electricity (D)
5. Big Bang Theory (E)
6. Periodic Table (D)
7. Capacitor (condenser) (C)
8. Quantum Theory (E)
9. Atomic Bomb (E)
10. Penicillin (E)
11. X-rays (D)

English

The procedure is the same as the one used above. When were each of these famous authors born? Choose from (A) before 1800 (B) 1800–1850 (C) 1851–1900 (D) 1901–1950

1. Ernest Hemingway (C)
2. Mark Twain (B)
3. William Shakespeare (A)
4. Stephen King (D)
5. Edgar Allan Poe (B)
6. William Faulkner (C)
7. F. Scott Fitzgerald (C)
8. Charles Dickens (B)
9. George Orwell (D)
10. Oscar Wilde (C)
11. James Joyce (C)
12. Virginia Woolf (C)
13. Ralph Waldo Emerson (B)
14. Ray Bradbury (D)
15. Agatha Christie (C)

16. Leo Tolstoy (B)
17. Lewis Carroll (B)
18. Walt Whitman (B)

Social Studies

The procedure is the same as the one used above. When did each of these famous events in U.S. history take place? Choose from (A) before 1600 (B) 1600–1799 (C) 1800–1899 (D) 1900–1949 (E) 1950–1999 (F) 2000–

1. Korean War (E)
2. President John F. Kennedy is assassinated in Dallas, Tex. (E)
3. Texan defenders of the Alamo are all killed during siege by the Mexican Army. (C)
4. World War I (D)
5. The United Nations is established. (D)
6. Vietnam War (E)
7. Barack Obama becomes the first African American to be elected president. (F)
8. Watergate cover-up (E)
9. Christopher Columbus, financed by Spain, makes the first of four voyages to the New World. (A)
10. Persian Gulf War (E)
11. The Plymouth Colony in Massachusetts is established by Pilgrims from England. (B)
12. Stock market crash precipitates the Great Depression. (D)
13. Civil War (C)
14. Japan attacks Pearl Harbor. (D)
15. Rev. Martin Luther King, Jr., is assassinated in Memphis, Tennessee. Senator Robert F. Kennedy is assassinated in Los Angeles, California. (E)
16. Two hijacked jetliners ram twin towers of World Trade Center in the worst terrorist attack against the United States. (F)
17. Space shuttle *Challenger* explodes seventy-three seconds after liftoff, killing all seven crew members. (E)
18. Astronauts Neil Armstrong and Edwin Aldrin Jr. become the first men to land on the Moon. (E)
19. Gold is discovered at Sutter's Mill in California; gold rush reaches its height the following year. (C)
20. American Revolution (B)

Math

Below is a list of famous mathematicians along with their place of birth. Following that is a list of important mathematical discoveries. For this game use either or both lists.

The procedure is the same as the one used above. When were each of these famous mathematicians born? Choose from (A) prior to the first century, (B) 1501–1600, (C) 1601–1700, (D) 1701–1800, (E) 1801–1900.

1. Johann Carl Friedrich Gauss, Germany (D)
2. Blaise Pascal, France (C)
3. Leonhard Euler, Switzerland (D)
4. Pythagoras of Samos, Greece (A)
5. George Pólya, Hungary (E)
6. Francesco Bonaventura de Cavalieri, Italy (B)
7. Leonhard Euler, Switzerland (D)
8. Georg Friedrich Bernhard Riemann, Germany (E)
9. Zeno of Elea, Greece (A)
10. Johannes Kepler, Germany (B)
11. Isaac (Sir) Newton, England (C)
12. Aristotle of Stagira, Macedonia (A)
13. Euclid of Megara & Alexandria, Greece (A)
14. John Napier, Scotland (B)
15. Archimedes, Greece (A)
16. Galileo Galilei, Italy (B)
17. René Déscartes, France (B)
18. Pierre de Fermat, France (C)
19. Gottfried Wilhelm von Leibniz, Germany (C)
20. Albert Einstein, Germany (E)

Important Mathematical Discoveries

When were these mathematical discoveries made? Choose from (A) prior to first century, (B) first century through 1499, (C) 1500 through 1699, (D) 1700 through 1899.

1. Indian numerals are modified by Arab mathematicians to form the modern Hindu-Arabic numeral system (used universally in the modern world). (B)
2. Abraham de Moivre introduces the normal distribution to approximate the binomial distribution in probability. (D)
3. The Pythagorean Theorem and irrational numbers are discovered. (A)

4. John Napier presents Napierian logarithms. (C)
5. The basis of trigonometry are developed. (A)
6. Rules are established for manipulating both negative and positive numbers, for computing square roots, and for solving linear and quadratic equations. (B)
7. The first known approximation of pi is computed to be 3.125. (A)
8. Al-Khwarizmi—Persian mathematician, father of algebra, writes the *Al-Jabr*, later transliterated as *Algebra*, which introduces systematic algebraic techniques for solving linear and quadratic equations. (B)
9. Carl Friedrich Gauss proves the fundamental theorem of algebra (every polynomial equation has a solution among the complex numbers). (D)
10. Law of Sines is discovered by Muslim mathematicians. (B)
11. Earliest known decimal system is developed. (A)
12. Ibn al-Banna and al-Qalasadi introduced symbolic notation for algebra. (B)
13. The earliest calculator, the abacus, is invented. (A)
14. René Descartes discovers analytic geometry and is the first to use the term "imaginary numbers." (C)
15. Equations higher than the second degree are first solved. (B)
16. Calculus is invented. (C)
17. Edmund Halley prepares the first mortality tables statistically relating death rate to age. (C)
18. Rules are developed for finding the volume of a sphere, and the formula for solving quadratic equations is established. (B)
19. Johann Heinrich Lambert proves that pi is irrational. (D)
20. Blaise Pascal and Pierre de Fermat create the theory of probability. (C)

Chapter Five

Stay Tuned for More Games

The following games are based on some popular TV game shows. Many students have watched some of these shows and have enjoyed them. Consequently, when they are played in the classroom, the students are enthusiastic and willing participants, which results in enhanced learning.

THE MESSAGE GAME (M, H)

This game is somewhat similar to *Wheel of Fortune*. It is typically played to go over homework, although it can be used for drill and practice. This is a team game, with the winning team earning a reward such as a treat or extra credit.

Procedure

- To begin, the students move into their regular cooperative learning groups. (If groups are not regularly used, they can be put together for the purposes of this game.) Assign a team spokesperson for each team, or have the team choose one.
- If the task is to go over homework, give the students a few minutes with their teammates to discuss the previous assignment in an attempt to reach consensus on the answers. While they are doing this, put blank spaces on the board (or overhead projector) that when filled in will form a short sentence or message. Some suggestions are on p. 35.
- List on the board all the team names in random order.
- After each team has indicated that they are ready to go, the game begins. The object of the game is to guess what the message is.

- To start, call on the team at the top of the list. Choose a problem/question and the team spokesperson gives the answer. If it is correct, that team chooses a letter (consonant or vowel) in an attempt to fill in one or more of the blank spaces. If the letter is part of one or more of the words, it is put into the blank space(s).
- After a team answers a problem/question correctly and selects a letter that is in the message, they may guess what the sentence says; no penalty for a wrong guess. If they are correct, they have won the game; if not, the turn passes to the next team on the list.
- If a team gives a wrong answer, the same question is given to the next team on the list. Neither the question nor the incorrect answer is repeated; it is each team's responsibility to pay attention to what is going on!
- Continue down the list of team names, calling on each team, until a correct answer is given. Again the team chooses a letter and, if correct, may try to guess the message. If they are not successful, go back to the list and pick the next team in order that has not had a first attempt at a problem.
- The procedure is continued until the message is guessed.

Notes

- Sometimes you may run out of homework questions before the game is completed. Consequently, it is wise to have some extra problems ready, perhaps from supplementary questions in the back of the book, such as from a chapter review or worksheet.
- Also, if time is running out and it is obvious that the game cannot be completed using the stated rules, simply fill in letters in the blank spaces, one at a time, and the first team to correctly state the message wins.

Some Suggested Messages

- Winners make commitments.
- If you believe it, you can achieve it.
- Quitters never win; winners never quit.
- To break a bad habit, drop it.
- We trip over pebbles, not mountains.
- Discipline yourself so others won't have to.
- Excuses are for losers.
- By failing to prepare, you are preparing to fail.
- Make an effort, not an excuse.
- Quitting is not an option.
- There is no excuse for abuse.

- Be yourself. Everyone else is taken.
- Time flies, but you're the pilot.

After the message is completed, it is interesting to ask the students what it means. This is a good opportunity to discuss some of the issues raised by the above statements.

Messages on the Lighter Side

- If you don't pay your exorcist, you get repossessed.
- When a clock is hungry, it goes back for seconds.
- Every calendar's days are numbered.
- A boiled egg in the morning is hard to beat.
- Once you've seen one shopping center, you've seen a mall.
- Acupuncture is a jab well done.
- Santa's helpers are subordinate clauses.
- Reading while sunbathing will make you well red.
- When two egotists meet, it's an I for an I.
- A backward poet writes inverse.

ONE VS. THE CLASS (M, H)

This game is similar to the TV game *1 vs. 100*. One student, who will be called the "One," competes against the rest of the class. This game can be used primarily for drill and practice.

Procedure:

- Give each student several pieces of paper.
- Randomly choose the "One" who stands in front of the room facing the class.
- The rest of the class is to stand up next to their desks.
- The teacher asks a question and gives the students an appropriate amount of time to write an answer on one of the pieces of paper.
- When everyone in the class is finished, the piece of paper is held up with the blank side facing the "One."
- The "One" then gives his/her answer and the rest of the class turns the paper around showing their answer to the teacher.
- If the answer given by the "One" is correct, he/she remains in front of the room and is awarded one point for each class member who got the answer incorrect.

- Any class member who gets a question wrong is eliminated from this round and must sit down.
- Play continues and another question is given. The "One" remains in front of the class until he/she gives a wrong answer. The "One" continues to accumulate points based on the number of classmates who give incorrect answers.
- If the "One" gives an incorrect answer, he/she now becomes part of the class and a new "One" is randomly chosen from the remaining students who got a correct answer.
- Any student who had previously been eliminated is now back in play (including the former "One").
- Play continues as described above.
- The winner is the "One" who accumulated the most points.

Since there can only be a few "Ones" in this game, some students may think it is not fair if they didn't have the opportunity to be the "One." Explain to the class that since the "One" was chosen at random, all had an equal chance of being selected.

JEOPARDY (M, H)

Jeopardy has been a very popular TV show for several decades. Many students enjoy watching and comparing their knowledge with that of the players on TV. Classroom Jeopardy takes advantage of this interest by students. This game can be used for drill and practice with a wide variety of subjects.

Materials needed: overhead projector; transparencies of Jeopardy game boards (samples are in the appendix); heavy cardboard or oak-tag squares to conceal answers.

Set Up

- Place a transparency of the Jeopardy game board (see appendix for sample boards) on the overhead projector.
- Place one or more "Daily Double" square(s), written on regular paper, over one or more of the questions.
- Cover all the questions with the cardboard squares.

Procedure

- Organize the class into two teams; let's call them Team A and Team B.

- Flip a coin to decide which team goes first; let's say it's Team A.
- Randomly select a member of Team A, who chooses the category and point value.
- Expose the question by lifting off the piece of cardboard, and allow the student an appropriate amount of time to come up with the answer. (Note: unlike the TV game, the board has questions, not answers.)
  ◊ If he/she is correct, the point value for that question is awarded to Team A and another randomly chosen member of Team A chooses a category and point value. Play continues until an incorrect answer is given.
  ◊ When that happens, randomly choose a member of Team B to answer the same question. If the correct answer is given, that point value is awarded to Team B and another randomly chosen member of Team B gets to pick the category and point value.
- The team to give the last correct answer chooses the category and point value.
- If a "Daily Double" square is exposed, the student may risk up to as much as the team has earned so far on the next question. A maximum of 50 points may be wagered if the team has accumulated less than that amount.
- The teacher should keep score on the board for all to see.
- Play continues for a predetermined time or until all the answers have been exposed.
- If you wish to have a "Final Jeopardy" round, follow the procedure below:
  ◊ Announce the Final Jeopardy category
  ◊ Randomly choose three members from each team. Each trio gets together and decides how much of their team's points will be wagered on the final question.
  ◊ Give a final question and allow the trios to discuss it before submitting a written answer to you along with the wager. If they get the correct answer, the amount of points bet is added to their score; if the answer is incorrect, the wager is subtracted from their score.
- When the game is over, points earned will be totaled, and the winning team can earn some kind of reward (extra credit, pencils, treats, an autographed photo of Alex Trebek, etc.).

If you have a "smart classroom" you may consider creating your own PowerPoint Jeopardy game. Go to Google and enter *Jeopardy templates* into the search box. You will be given access to several sites that allow you to download PowerPoint Jeopardy templates. Go through the sites until you find one you like. Then follow the directions to create your own PowerPoint Jeopardy board. Also consider adding some special effects by including the Jeopardy theme music and the sound made when a "Daily Double" is exposed. It does take time to create your board, but once it is done you have it for many years to come.

After your board is set up, you can use the procedure given above to play PowerPoint Jeopardy with your class.

There are many free Jeopardy templates available online. Prep time for the game becomes more manageable if you take advantage of these materials. You could also consider making a project for small groups of students to create their own Jeopardy game. They choose the categories, the questions, and the point values.

PASSWORD (M, H)

Most kids may not know the TV game show *Password*, so it may need more explanation. This classroom game is an adaptation of that popular TV game show.

Procedure

- Randomly select two students to be the "contestants."
- Those two students go to the front of the room and face the class.
- Write the password on the board or hold up a card with the password on it. Everyone should be able to see the password *except* the two contestants.
- The rest of the students raise their hands to offer one-word clues to the contestants that might help them guess the word.
- Each contestant takes turns calling on their classmates until one of the contestants correctly guesses the password. Each contestant is limited to a maximum of three students to call on.
- If the contestant who guesses the password does so after one clue, three points are awarded; after two clues, two points are awarded; after three clues, one point is awarded. The contestant who guesses the password remains at the front of the class and continues to play. The student who gave the clue which allowed the contestant to guess the password, replaces the other contestant.

By carefully choosing words appropriate for your students' abilities, this game can be played with a wide variety of classes and levels of students. It is best to use words for which students might know many meanings. For example the password *enormous* might be gotten from such clues as *big, huge, large, great, bulky, hefty*. Before playing the game you may wish to use a dictionary or thesaurus to create a list of possible words. If you write those words on cards, use large letters so students can easily see them. These cards can be saved and used year after year.

FAMILY FEUD (M, H)

Procedure

- Randomly create two teams of five students.
- Seat each team in their own row.
- Have a randomly chosen player from each of those two teams come to the front of the room and stand on either side of a designated desk that has two inverted cups on it.
- Give a statement like "Name five of the six New England states."
- Whoever taps the cup first gets to respond, along with his/her team.
- Beginning with the "tapper," each team member, in turn and without help from teammates, names a New England state.
- Each team member is awarded one point for each correct answer.
- After this turn is over, randomly create two more teams of five and randomly choose one player from each team to come to the front of the room. (Randomly creating new teams gives each student an equal chance of playing.)
- Play continues as described above.
- Score can be kept on a classroom list of students.
- The three students that scores the most points are winners.

Some Possible Categories

English: Name five parts of speech; name five punctuation marks.
Science: Name five planets in our solar system; name five categories of rocks.
Math: Name five polygons; name five prime numbers between 30 and 60.
Social Studies: Name five presidents who were in office after 1970; name five of the eight states that begin with the letter *N*.

Chapter Six

Assembly Required

These games require some preparation time. However, once the work has been done, you have these materials to use over and over again. These games are more sophisticated than most of the other games in this book, and the students really seem to enjoy them. Consequently, they are worth the effort.

BINGO! (E, M, H)

Bingo is a game we often begin to play in our childhood and continue to play well into our senior years. There is an old riddle which goes something like this. How do you get a senior citizen to yell an obscene four-letter word? Answer: get a senior citizen sitting nearby to yell "Bingo!"

Here are some ways to prepare for classroom bingo.

- You can buy a bingo game from an educational supply store. Since teaching is not among the highest-paid professions, you will likely not want to spend your money on this; and since school budgets are usually tight, you may want to consider another approach.
- You can create the bingo cards yourself. Just make sure all the cards are arranged differently from each other. This does take some prep time, but once it is done, you have the cards to use for many years, especially if they are laminated.
- If you have older, more responsible students, you can have them help in the preparation.
  ◊ Get a copy of a standard bingo card and convert it into a blank card. Do this by covering up the numbers by taping a small piece of paper over each of the printed numbers.

◊ Or you can simply make a card with a pen and ruler.
◊ In either case, run off copies, preferably on heavy-duty paper such as oak tag.
◊ Then have each student randomly fill in the squares from a list of clues you read or from a word/number bank. Make sure each student's card is different from the rest.

- If you don't want to buy plastic markers to cover the cells on the bingo cards, cut-up pieces of construction paper will do. Be careful about using objects such as small rocks or coins for markers; they easily can become guided missiles.

Sample Cards

For *Social Studies* Bingo, the card could be filled with famous dates, names of historical characters, historically significant events, or a combination of these or other topics. As an example, the clue might be to say "He was the president who abolished slavery." The students (hopefully) cover "Abraham Lincoln."

For *Language Arts* Bingo, the clues could be the definitions of various words that appear on the bingo card. Read the definitions and the kids have to match them up with the word being defined. For example, you say "a person, place, thing, or idea" and the students cover up "noun."

For *Math* Bingo, the card can be filled with numbers that are answers to various simple problems you read as clues. For example, you might ask the students to round 435.67 to the nearest tenth. The students are required to cover 435.7.

For *Science* Bingo, you give the definition of, or describe a word from your unit of study. For example, you might say, "It is the largest planet in our solar system" and the correct response would be for the students to cover "Jupiter."

TEAM TOURNAMENT (M, H)

The Team Tournament is a student favorite. They will often ask to play it. It provides an important lesson about the value of teamwork. The aspects of helping others and then being individually accountable to your team transcend the specific topics or concepts actually used in the game. It can be used for drill and practice on various topics and skills.

Initially it requires some work to get the materials ready, but once they are prepared, you have most of them to use many times during a year or career.

Preparing for the Tournament

Students are divided into heterogeneous cooperative learning teams to prepare for a competitive tournament. During the intergroup competition, the students individually compete against members of about the same ability level from other teams. The teams whose members do the best in competition earn some type of reward (extra credit, pens, etc.).

Materials needed:

- Each student will need a problem sheet, a challenge sheet, appropriate tools (pencil, calculator, etc.)
- Each competitive group will need a pack of number squares (preferably color coded, for easier sorting), consisting of numbers representing each problem to be done; two "double-point value" squares and one "triple-point value" square; one score card; one answer sheet; scrap paper.

After you have covered the subject matter, assign students to learning teams of three to five members. (If cooperative learning groups are normally used, assigning new learning teams is unnecessary.) Give them study questions/problems similar to those that will be used during the competition. Teammates study together, attempting to prepare each member for competition, because the chances of winning are greatly increased if all team members are well prepared.

The team tournament is held, usually the next day.

The Tournament

- Assign team members to a group to compete against members of about the same ability level from the other teams. Use previous grades and/or your personal judgment to construct the competitive groups.
- Group members are to determine roles of scorer and timekeeper.
- Give each player a sheet of questions and a challenge sheet.
- Give each group a set of number squares (see "materials needed" above), a score card, an answer sheet, and scrap paper.
- Instruct each group to spread out the number squares facedown on the desk. Each player draws a number, the highest going first. Once that is decided, the player to the right of this person is given the answer sheet, which should be placed facedown. Play rotates clockwise.
- The player whose turn it is draws a number square that indicates the question to be done on the question sheet. Each question is worth one point. If a double- or triple-score square is drawn, the value of the question is either

two or three points respectively, and the player draws again. All players attempt to answer this question.

- Before the time limit is reached, usually thirty to sixty seconds, the player must give an answer. The scorer asks if there are any challenges. All players wishing to challenge (including the scorer and person with the answer sheet) must write what they feel is the correct answer on the challenge sheet. All challenges are then shown simultaneously. The person with the answer sheet then looks up the correct answer.
- If the player who originally answered the question is correct, he/she scores 1 point (more if a double- or triple-point value square has been previously drawn). If he/she is incorrect the score is 0. If a player is unable to do a problem, or is unable to answer within the time limit, his/her score is 0, and the challenge procedure is then in effect. All correct challenges earn the point value of that question, while all incorrect challenges lose the point value.
- After the scorekeeper records the scores for that round, play (and the answer sheet) rotates clockwise.
- Play continues until a predetermined time or number of rounds is reached.
- Once the game is over, the scorekeeper fills in the "Points Earned" column on the score card and returns it to you. Your task is to determine tournament points for each team as follows:
  ◊ If two students from the same team are in the same competitive group, their points earned are averaged and they count as one person.
  ◊ If there are n people in a group, the person finishing with the highest number of points earned is awarded n tournament points for his team. The second highest number of earned points is awarded $n - 1$ tournament points for his/her team, and so on.
  ◊ You then add up the total number of tournament points earned by each team to determine the final standings. If the original teams do not have the same number of players in competition, the tournament points earned are averaged to determine the final standings.

In the appendix are copies of a blank challenge sheet and score card and a number array. These can be reproduced and used to play. For durability, the numbers should be reproduced on oak tag, or some other heavy-duty paper (for easy sorting, colored paper is recommended). Also, there is a sample score sheet, which should help explain the scoring process.

You and your students may struggle with this game the first time you play it; that is not uncommon. The next time you play it, begin by reviewing the rules and ask if the students have any questions. Having gone through it once, the students have a much better understanding of the rules and the flow of the game, and usually have little or no trouble. The more they play it, the more smoothly it runs.

CASINO DAY (M, H)

Gambling seems to be common in our culture. The NCAA basketball bracket, which millions fill out during "March Madness"; weekly bets on football and basketball games; and World Series and Super Bowl pools are all very normal in today's society, even among our students. Preaching to students about the possible pitfalls of gambling usually falls on deaf ears. This activity heightens the students' awareness that when you gamble, the game is not always fair and most of the time, those who bet lose. In casino-type games, in the long run, the house always wins; it has to or it goes out of business. The lesson learned here will hopefully be remembered by students throughout their lives.

Casino Day is intended as an activity for a math class, but it could be used as a lesson in most disciplines. The math involved is not difficult, and the students should enjoy this hands-on activity, which is exciting, entertaining, and educational.

Although this activity is better suited for older students, with some modifications it can be used with the younger students as well. Begin a day or two in advance by explaining to your students what you are planning. Invite students to help collect the materials needed (see below).

Overview: Games of chance are common in our society. But are the games we play or see played fair? In general, when people gamble, do they have a fair chance of winning? To help to answer these questions, the students are going to participate in a Casino Day, during which they will play and analyze some simple games of chance.

Objective: To determine which of several games played are fair games.

Room Setup: Move all but five desks to the perimeter of the room. This allows for easy movement of the players from station to station. Set up the five desks as gambling stations for each of the five games: (1) Two Dice Game—Sums, (2) Two Dice Game—Products, (3) Chips Ahoy, (4) The Great Race, and (5) Random Faces. Each of these games will be operated by those students who are playing the role of the House. Ask for volunteers or choose five responsible students to play this role.

Materials needed:

- five dice
- four chips (two of one color and two of another, preferably red and white) and a small bag or box

- six tiny racers (animals, cars, etc.) and a race track (see appendix)
- one deck of cards
- play money, bought or homemade (see appendix)
- score cards and game analysis sheets for each student (answers are in the appendix)
- one set of game rules for each station

Procedure

You will need an entire class period to complete this activity.

- At the beginning of class on Casino Day, explain the rules of the games that will be played at each of the five stations. For convenience, number the stations. Depending on the level of the class, you may want to demonstrate how each of the games is played. If you feel the students who are playing the role of the House are capable, allow them to go to their respective station and explain the rules of the game he/she will be conducting. For quick reference, copies of the game rules should be available at each station.
- If not already done, assign each student who volunteered to play the role of the House to a game station. Give this student a score card and $20 in play money. (It may be necessary to give the House additional money later on in the class.)
- Assign about equal numbers of players to each of the five game stations. Give each player a score card and $10 of play money. Also determine a rotation order so that each student knows where he/she is going next. (You don't want to have too many students at one station at the same time.) For example, you might say to the players that when they complete game 1, move on to game 2; when they complete game 2, move on to game 3; and so on. (When they complete game 5, move on to game 1.) It is a good idea to write this plan on the board or at each station.
- The players place wagers ($1 bets) using play money. If the player wins, the House gives back the bet for that particular game plus the appropriate payoff. If the player loses, the House keeps the wager.
- Each player will carry a score card and pencil to keep track of the results. If you wish, students can turn in the score cards to you so you can compile the class-wide results and report back to the class at a later time.
- After playing all five games, players may play additional games if time permits. Allow time at the end of class for each student to complete the Games Analysis sheet. (*Depending on the level of your class, you may consider supplying the students with the sample spaces called for in the first three games. See Games Analysis Answers in the appendix.*) If time is

short, the Games Analysis sheet can be completed for homework. Students should put their name on the sheet and hand it in to you. These sheets could be used as an assessment.

The Games

Note: When the player wins a bet, the original bet is returned plus the winnings from the bet.

Two Dice Games — Sums

Bet $1 play money per roll.
  Rules:

- Roll both dice. Add the two numbers. Do this twenty times. Keep a tally of odd and even sums.
- Player wins $1 from the House if the sum is odd.
- Player loses $1 to House if the sum is even.
- The payoff takes place after twenty rolls have been completed.
- The payoff is the difference between the number of even sums and odd sums.

Two Dice Games — Products

Bet $1 play money per roll.
  Rules:

- Roll both dice. Multiply the two numbers. Do this twenty times. Keep a tally of odd and even products.
- Player wins $1 from the House if the product is odd.
- Player loses $1 to House if the product is even.
- The payoff takes place after twenty rolls have been completed.
- The payoff is the difference between the number of even products and odd products.

Chips Ahoy

Bet $1 play money per draw.
  Rules:

- The House places two red and two white chips in a box or bag.
- The player draws two chips without replacement.

- If both chips the player draws are the same color, the player wins $1 from the House.
- If the player draws two different color chips, he/she loses $1 to the House.
- There are to be twenty draws from the bag/box. After each draw, the player drops the drawn chips into the bag, the House holds the bag by the top, shakes it, and then the player reaches in to draw the chips.
- Keep a tally of the outcomes. The payoff occurs after twenty draws are made.

The Great Race

See the appendix for a model race track, or you can construct one yourself or have a student do it. Let him/her add graphics (flags, racing cars, etc.) to personalize the track.

Bet $1 play money per racer.

Rules:

- Six racers (tiny toy animals, cars, etc.) are put in the starting gates at the beginning of each of six lanes.
- Each player bets on one or more racers.
- All six racers must be bet on.
- A die is rolled by the House. The number on the die indicates one forward move of the racer in that lane.
- The first racer to cross the finish line wins.
- The winning racer receives $3 in play money from the House.

Random Faces

Bet $1 play money per draw

Rules:

- The House shuffles a deck of cards and spreads them facedown on a desk.
- The player draws one card.
- If the drawn card is a face card—Jack, Queen, or King, the player wins $3 from the House.
- If any other card is drawn, the player loses his/her $1 to the House.
- Play the game ten times. Keep a tally of the results.
- The payoff occurs after ten draws have been made.

Casino Games Score Card

Name_____

Circle one: I am a Player/the House

If you are a Player, carry this sheet with you from game to game and fill it out as you go along. You need to record the results for all the players and the House, so do not leave the station until all the players have had a turn. If you are the House, keep score and results as the Players come to you.

Two Dice Games—Sums

Number of Player wins   Tally: _____ Total: _____

Number of House wins   Tally: _____ Total: _____

Overall, for this game, the Players won/lost $ _____

Overall, for this game, the House won/lost $ _____

Two Dice Games—Products

Number of Player wins   Tally: _____ Total: _____

Number of House wins   Tally: _____ Total: _____

Overall, for this game, the Players won/lost $ _____

Overall, for this game, the House won/lost $ _____

Chips Ahoy

Number of Player wins   Tally: _____ Total: _____

Number of House wins   Tally: _____ Total: _____

Overall, for this game, the Players won/lost $ _____

Overall, for this game, the House won/lost $ _____

The Great Race

Total amount of money won by *all* the Players $ _____

Total amount of money won by the House $ _____

Random Faces

Number of Player wins   Tally: _____ Total: _____

Number of House wins   Tally: _____ Total: _____

Overall, for this game, the Players won/lost $ _____

Overall, for this game, the House won/lost $ _____

Answer these after you have completed all 5 games.

At the beginning of the class, how much money did you have? $_____

After you completed all the games, how much money did you have? $_____

That means you won/lost $ _____

Note to the teacher: answers for the games analysis are in the appendix.

Casino Day—Games Analysis

Name _____ Class _____
Date_____
These sheets are to be neatly completed and handed in by the end of class.
Objective: To determine which of the games played on Casino Day are *fair*
games.
The following definitions will help in the analysis:

- A game is *fair* if each player has an equal chance of winning.
- The *probability* of winning is the number of favorable outcomes divided by
  the total number of possible outcomes. As an example, let's say you win
  a bet if you roll a die and get a number less than 3. This probability is the
  number of favorable outcomes, that is 2 (rolling a 1 or 2), divided by the
  total number of possible outcomes, that is 6 (rolling a 1, 2, 3, 4, 5, or 6). So
  the probability of rolling a die and getting a number less than 3 is 2/6 or 1/3.

Reminder: When the player wins a bet, he/she has his/her original bet
returned *plus* the winnings from the bet.
Before answering the questions below, it would be wise to review the rules
of each game.

Two Dice Game—Sums

1. In the area to the right, create a sample space for all possible sums when
   rolling two dice.
2. What is the probability of rolling an odd sum? _____
3. What is the probability of rolling an even sum? _____
4. Is this a fair game? Why?

Two Dice Game—Products

1. In the area to the right, create a sample space for all possible products
   when rolling two dice.
2. What is the probability of rolling an odd product? _____
3. What is the probability of rolling an even product? _____
4. Is this a fair game? Why?

Chips Ahoy

1. Make a sample space of the possible outcomes. Hint: Think of the chips as red chip #1, red chip #2, white chip #1, and white chip #2. Use the following notation: Rl, R2, Wl, and W2.
2. What is the probability of Rl, R2 on successive draws? _____ (note that R2, Rl is the same outcome)
3. What is the probability of W1, W2 on successive draws? _____
4. Is this a fair game? Why?

The Great Race

1. How many possible outcomes are there? _____
2. What is the probability of racer #1 winning? _____
3. What is the probability of racer #2 winning? _____
4. What is the probability of racer #3 winning? _____
5. What is the probability of racer #4 winning? _____
6. What is the probability of racer #5 winning? _____
7. What is the probability of racer #6 winning? _____
8. Assuming all 6 racers were bet on, how much does the House initially collect? After paying off the winner, has the House won or lost? _____ How much? _____
9. Does every racer have an equal chance of winning? _____
10. If you consider player against player only, is this a fair game? _____ Why? _____
11. In this game, can the House lose? _____ Explain. _____
    _____

Random Faces

1. How many possible outcomes are there? (Hint: How many different cards can be selected; suit doesn't matter.) _____
2. What is the probability of drawing a Jack or Queen or King? _____
3. If you play this game thirteen times, how many times should you expect to win?
4. After having played the game thirteen times, you should expect to have (choose one) won/lost $_____
5. Considering that you are playing against the House, is this a fair game? _____
6. Why? _____

After analyzing the five games played on Casino Day, what conclusion(s) have you come to? (Use an additional sheet of paper if necessary.)

CLASSROOM OLYMPICS (M, H)

This is a good activity to provide drill and practice on important topics; it is particularly useful as a review session, especially before a unit test, a mid-term, or final exam.
  Procedure:

- Decide on the topics you are going to use and organize them into four "events." For example, in a math class the events could be (1) applying the laws of exponents, (2) factoring, (3) solving linear equations, and (4) operations with polynomials. Topics in an English class could be (1) grammar, (2) spelling, (3) punctuation, and (4) vocabulary. Events for a social studies class may be (1) The Civil War, (2) politics, (3) current events, and (4) presidents. Candidates for science events might be (1) our solar system, (2) plants, (3) animals, and (4) simple machines.
- On the day before the competition, organize the students into groups of three or four; balance the groups so that each has about the same number of strong, average, and weak students. If you normally use cooperative learning groups, they can be the teams for the competition.
- Then give each student a listing of practice problems (and answers) from a worksheet or textbook. For honors-level classes, you can require the students to come up with the answers on their own. Students will be given time to work in their teams to prepare each other for the games, as there will be individual awards as well as team awards.
- On the day of the competition, each student will be given his/her event (not knowing the event until now forces each student to prepare in all areas). All students in the same event will go head-to-head in elimination brackets (similar to the ones used in the NCAA basketball tournament). (Follow a procedure similar to the one found in the Survive and Advance game on page 62.) The top three finishers in each event will earn 3, 2, and 1 extra credit points, respectively.
- First-place finishers will earn 3 points for their teams, second-place finishers 2 points, and third-place finishers, 1 point. Each member of the top three finishing teams will be awarded 3, 2, and 1 additional extra credit points, respectively.
- You can also consider making individual gold, silver, and bronze paper medals (graphics from a computer) for the top three finishers in each event, as well as gold, silver, and bronze paper trophies for the top three teams. These awards can be displayed on a bulletin board in the classroom for all to see. Consequently, many students who normally are not successful in class will have their "moment in the sun."

Chapter Seven

But Wait . . . There's More!

This chapter contains a diverse variety of games. You are sure to find something engaging for students at every level.

IT'S IN THE CARDS (E, M, H)

You will need several decks of standard playing cards to play the next three games listed below. Request the students to ask their relatives and friends for decks that may have missing or torn cards. Also ask your teaching colleagues for old decks they are willing to part with. Complete decks are not necessary for this game. Remove the face cards (Jacks, Queens, and Kings) from the decks. The objective in these is to give the students practice in mental arithmetic.

Math Wars (E)

Materials needed: one deck of cards (as described above) for each pair of students. As an alternative to cards, write the numbers from 1 to 10 on small tabs of paper.
  Procedure:

- Have students work in pairs
- Each student draws two cards from the deck and multiplies them together.
- If you want the students to have practice with addition facts, let them add the card values.
- The highest answer wins the cards.

- Once they have gone through all the cards in the deck, the student with the most cards is the winner.
- Have students change partners, and play continues as described.

Multiplication Baseball (E, M)

Materials needed: cards or number tabs as described on p. 53; a drawing of a baseball diamond; three coins or some other markers to represent the base runners.
 Procedure:

- Have students work in pairs.
- Flip a coin to decide who bats first.
- This player draws two cards from the deck and multiplies them together.
- If his/her answer is incorrect, an out is recorded. If the answer is correct, the player moves his/her markers around the baseball diamond according to the following products:
  ◊ 27–48 is a single
  ◊ 50–60 is a double
  ◊ 63, 70, or 72 is a triple
  ◊ 80 or 90 is a homerun
  ◊ 2–24 is an out
- The cards (or tabs) are shuffled or mixed up, and the at bat continues.
- The players keep track of the runs scored and the number of outs.
- The player's turn continues until he/she records three outs.
- After three outs, the other player is now the batter, and play continues until a predetermined number of innings have been played or a time limit is reached.
- The player who scored the most runs is the winner.

Equations (M, H)

Materials needed: cards or number tabs as described.
 Procedure:

- Arrange the students into small groups of four or five students sitting in a circle.
- One student deals four cards to form a 2 × 2 square, and then a fifth card to the side of that square. As an example, see below.

$$5 \quad 3$$
$$8$$
$$2 \quad A$$

- Each card has its own face value, with an ace being 1.
- The students must use each of the four cards in the 2 × 2 square exactly once in the operations of addition, subtraction, multiplication, and/or division to write an expression that equals the value of the fifth card. Order of operations is not important. For the above example: $(5 + 3) \times (2 - 1) = 8$
- The first person to state the correct answer wins a point. The student can hold the cards instead of keeping score.
- With classes that have studied square roots, that may also be used.

Note: there is not always a solution, or a solution may be very difficult to find. For challenging arrays of numbers, consider giving interested students an opportunity to work on a solution out of class.

FAST FACTS (E, M, H)

This game can be used at any level with any discipline. The difficulty of the categories will need to be appropriate for the students involved. Objective: drill and practice.

Procedure:

- Begin by assigning three students to be judges. These students are to write the categories and will judge the order of finish of the players.
- Divide the rest of the class into three teams of about equal numbers.
- One person randomly selected from each team comes to the board and picks up a marker.
- One of the judges then orally announces the category; for example, name any three of the six New England states; or name four famous American authors; or name any three parts of a flower. Simple math problems can also be used.
- As quickly as they can, the students write their responses on the board.
- The first one to correctly finish is awarded 3 points; the next to correctly finish receives 2 points; the last to correctly finish gets 1 point. The judges decide the order of finish. To receive points all the answers must be correct.
- The three players then return to their teams and another player from each team replaces them.
- A score keeper can be assigned (preferably a player who has completed his/her turn) to write the scores on the board; or score can be kept by the teacher.
- Once each player has had a turn, the scores are totaled and the team with the most points wins.

OFF THE WALL (M, H)

This is probably more of an activity than a game, but it can be very effective as a review, especially before a test.
   Procedure:

- Begin by writing several words or topics from your unit of study; for example, in a science course you might use moon, eclipse, tides, comets, and sun. Write each one at the top of a large piece of paper.
- Tape the papers to the walls around the room.
- Organize the students into as many groups as there are topics.
- Provide each group of students with a marker (different colors if possible to indicate which group wrote which comment).
- When you say "go" each group goes to a different paper and writes down everything they know about the word or topic.
- Depending on the topics and the class, decide on a time limit and when that limit is reached, instruct the students to rotate to the next paper and write anything they think is missing.
- Collect the papers after all the students are finished.
- One at a time, display them in the front of the room.
- Together read through what has been written.
- Add any important information that may have been missed, and if necessary, correct any inaccurate information.

FROM TOP TO BOTTOM (E, M, H)

This too is, perhaps, not as much a game as an activity. It can be used for review, similar to Off The Wall, but it is done on an individual basis.
   Procedure:

- Instruct the students to draw a horizontal line about midway between the top and bottom of a piece of paper.
- Write a comment or question on the board such as, "List as many punctuation marks as you can" or "Name all the presidents who served since the year 1980."
- Give students an appropriate amount of time to respond to the prompt. Tell them to write their answers on the top half of the paper.
- Ask several students to go to the board and write their responses; eliminate duplicate answers.

- Ask those students sitting at their seats to put check marks next to those responses on their papers that match what is written on the board.
- Tell students to write the answers from the board that they don't have on the top half of their paper on the bottom half.

DECEIVING DEFINITIONS (M, H)

Materials needed: a small pad; a list of words whose definitions will not be known by students.

Procedure:

- Turn around four desks so that they face the class.
- Randomly choose four students to occupy those desks; let's call them the panel.
- Give each of those students a piece of paper from a small pad.
- Choose one of the words from the list and write it on the board.
- Write the definition on a piece of paper from the same small pad.
- Each member of the panel is to write their name on the piece of paper and then make up a definition for the word.
- The teacher collects all the definitions and adds the real definition to the pile.
- The teacher then reads all five definitions for consideration of the rest of the class. Remind them that only one of the five is the actual definition.
- Read the definitions one more time and then ask the students to vote, by raising their hands, for the definition they think is the real one.
- Record the number of votes for each definition on each piece of paper with the made-up definitions.
- Scoring:
  ◊ A panel member receives one point for each student who votes for his/her definition.
  ◊ Class members receive two points if they choose the correct definition.
  ◊ A class member receives three points if he/she is the only one in class to choose the correct definition.
- Now randomly choose four new panel members, and play continues as described above.
- The winner is the student with the most points at the end of the game.

You may be amazed at how many of these words are in the dictionary.

Sample words:

ambatch (am-batch): spongy wood, often used for rafts.

dowitcher (dow-itch-urr): a long-legged North American bird.

chermany (churr-man-nee): a type of baseball played in the southern United States.

upanga (oo-pang-gah): a small flute played with the nose.

limosis (lye-mo-siss): an urgent desire to eat chalk.

PASS THE BUCK! (E, M)

Materials needed: a toy deer (buck), a picture of a buck, or a play money one-dollar bill; a list of topics (see below).

Procedure:

- Sit all the students in a circle.
- Randomly select one to be "It." This student holds the buck.
- The teacher now says to "It," for example, "Name five vegetables. Pass the buck."
- "It" now passes the buck to the right and the students pass the buck around the circle.
- If the buck returns to "It" before he/she names five vegetables, "It" remains "It."
- If "It" completes the list before the buck is returned to him/her, then the student holding the buck when the list is completed becomes the new "It."

Topics can be associated with your curriculum or can be general in nature. Some suggested topics:

- Circus animals
- Superheroes
- Birds
- Things associated with Halloween
- Fish
- Flowers
- Things associated with Thanksgiving
- baseball teams
- cartoon characters
- cereals
- states east of the Mississippi River
- states west of the Mississippi River
- Things associated with winter

- candy bars
- presidents of the United States
- animals found in the forest

PICTIONARY (E, M, H)

Pictionary is an engaging way to review a wide variety of topics.
Materials needed: three groups of notecards; on each is a concept or definition; cards are structured into three levels of difficulty: easy (1 point), medium (2 points), and difficult (3 points).
   Procedure:

- Organize the class into teams of three to five students.
- Randomly choose a team that gets to pick the level of card they will be working with.
- Randomly choose a member of that team who goes to the board; call him/her the "drawer."
- The "drawer" has one minute to draw pictures in an attempt to get his/her team to guess the concept or word on the card. The drawer cannot use symbols, letters, or numbers. If this is done, the team loses its turn and scores zero. The card is then passed on to another team and play continues.
- If the team makes a correct guess within one minute, they earn the point value associated with the level of the card: 1, 2, or 3 points.
- Then another team and drawer are chosen and play continues as described above.
- It may be necessary to institute the rule that if another team says the word or concept out loud, the team whose turn it is automatically is awarded the point value of the card.
- Also, while a turn is in progress, if another team makes excessive noise or is rude, they are penalized 1 point.
- Score should be kept at the board. The team earning the most points wins.

   Some suggested words:

Level 1	Level 2	Level 3
octopus	guitar	deer
telephone	igloo	engagement ring
top sign	dog	dragon
apple	flower	bee
balloon	door	music
tree	train	wand

TWENTY-ONE (E, M)

This game is good for practice with simple addition. Materials needed: Enough sets of number tabs for each pair of students. The tabs are numbered from 1 to 6 (see appendix).
  Procedure:

• Arrange students in pairs. (If there are an odd number of students in the class, there can be one group of three.)
• Each player has only one turn. During a turn, the player places all number tabs facedown and mixes them up.
• The player then turns over the numbers one by one. The student adds up the numbers as they are turned over. The object is to get a sum of 21 or as close to 21 without going over.
• A player may stop at any point and keep that score.
• After the turn is over, all the numbers are turned facedown and mixed up for the next player.
• If the sum is exactly 21, the player is awarded 25 points. If less than 21, the player's score is the sum of the numbers. If more than 21, the player's score is 0.
• Play continues for a predetermined number of turns or until a predetermined time limit is reached.
• The player with the highest score wins.

ROTATING ROWS (M, H)

This is a game for teams of three or four members, primarily used for drill and practice.
  This version consists of six teams, four having four members and the remaining two having three members. (For larger classes, appropriate adjustments should be made.) For simplicity, let's call the teams A, B, C, D, E, and F. Team members are then designated by a number, so "A1" is the first member of team A, and so on.
  Procedure:

• To begin, students are seated in rows by team. You can assign a name to each team or have them choose one. Each student has paper, pencil, and any tools (calculator, ruler, etc.) necessary for the questions to be answered.
• A question is written on the board/overhead projector or indicated from a page in the textbook or from a worksheet. The first three players from

each team, that is, A1, A2, A3; B1, B2, B3; and so on, are to answer the question; an appropriate time limit is usually given. (Note: at this point, the fourth players from teams A–D are only spectators.)

- When the time is up, all players put down their pencils and raise the papers with the answer.
- The teacher looks at all the papers, beginning with player 1 from each team. If player 1 has a correct solution, including the work clearly shown or an explanation (if applicable), his/her team is awarded 3 points. If the solution is incorrect, player 2's work is considered; if he/she has the correct solution, 2 points are awarded to the team; if player 2 is incorrect, player 3 can earn 1 point for the team with a correct solution.
- At the end of this first round, team scores are posted and the game continues.
- Now a question is given that is to be answered by players 2–4 of each team. For teams with only three members, player 1 must also assume the role of player 4. The same scoring rules apply.
- For the next round, players 3, 4, and 1, in that order (or players 3, 1, and 2 for teams of three) participate.
- Play as many rounds as time will allow, but leave time for one final round.
- At this point in the game, teammates are given one to two minutes to consult with each other. They must decide how many of the points they have earned they wish to wager on the final question. On a piece of paper containing the team name, the wager is written and given to the teacher. The final question is answered by one member of each team chosen at random.
- After the final scores are tallied, the top team(s) is/are given a reward that has been previously determined: extra credit or small prizes.

Note: To save time, you should determine seating arrangements and the final round participants prior to the beginning of class. Choosing the final-round participants at random increases the chances of teammates helping each other in the days leading up to this competition.

SURVIVE AND ADVANCE (M, H)

This activity is primarily used for drill and practice. It can be done on an individual basis, or as a team competition. It is a good activity to give students practice in thinking under pressure. Students are especially receptive to this game while the NCAA basketball tournament (March Madness) is in progress.

Procedure:

- Begin by randomly placing as many students who will be participating in a bracket similar to the one used in elimination tournaments. (Brackets can be found at Google Images/brackets.) If there are not enough students to fill the entire bracket, fill in the empty position(s) with the word *bye*, and the person randomly paired with "bye" automatically advances to the next round.
- Students participate two at a time. The two contestants can stay in their regular seats or come to the front of the room and occupy two seats designated for the competitors.
- To begin the competition, the teacher indicates which question the students will be doing. Questions might be from the textbook, a worksheet, a projection on the board, or even flash cards. The questions should be relatively easy and have a relatively short answer so that they can be answered in a few seconds; this will make it easier to determine who completes the answer first.
- Once the question is revealed the two contestants verbally give an answer. Pencil and paper may be used, if applicable. The first person to complete the correct answer is awarded 1 point. If both contestants give the correct answer, the one to state the complete answer first is the winner. (You may have to ask for help from the other students in class to determine who finished giving the answer first. If it's too close to call, disregard this question and go on to another one.)
- If the first person to respond is incorrect, his/her opponent is given five seconds to give an answer. If the answer is correct, 1 point is awarded; if the answer is incorrect, neither contestant scores, another question is given, and play continues. The first student to score 2 points advances to the next round.
- This procedure continues until everyone is eliminated except the ultimate winner.
- You can give extra credit to those who get to the final four, with additional credit given to the two finalists and still more to the winner.

INTERCLASS COMPETITION (M, H)

If you and a colleague teach the same course at the same time, you may want to consider this competition, which can take place in one of your classrooms. If the combined classes are too large, check to see if a bigger room is available during that period. Sit down with your colleague to discuss the rules and the type of problems/questions you will use. Once that is decided, choose a date for the contest and inform your students about the competition. Explain the rules of the game and then allow your students to choose captains for your team.

On the day of the competition, once all the students are in the same room, have your class sit on one side and your colleague's class on the other. Before play begins, announce the following:

- If a student other than those participating on the question yells out an answer, his/her team automatically forfeits the point.
- Inappropriate comments, excessive noise, or any other unsportsmanlike behavior will receive one warning; on each subsequent occurrence, a point will be deducted from the team's score.

Now review the rules to the students and you are ready to begin.
Game rules:

- One student from each class, chosen at random, will come to the front of the room and sit in designated seats.
- A question will be projected onto the screen from an overhead projector or computer.
- All students will work out the problem on paper. The two chosen students are the only ones who may verbally give an answer. The first person to *finish* giving the answer will get first consideration. (Note: For the answer to a math problem to be correct, appropriate units and any stated degree of accuracy must be included.) A correct answer earns 1 point for the team. If an incorrect answer is given, the opponent has five seconds to give an answer. If correct, 1 point is earned for that team.
- If both contestants give the wrong answer, two more students, one from each team, chosen at random, will be called upon. These students submit their written work to one of the officials (teacher). If the students show the correct answer and work (if appropriate), 1 point will be earned for their respective teams. If neither student gives a correct solution, two more students will be randomly chosen and play continues until someone displays the correct solution. This procedure increases the chances of all students working on the problem.
- A scoreboard will be kept for all to see.
- With about five minutes left, the previously chosen captains of each team will meet and decide how many of the earned points they wish to wager. The wager along with the team name will be submitted to an official.

- A final problem/question will then be projected. Only the captains may work on this. If the captains are correct, the points wagered are added to the team's total; if the answer is incorrect, the points will be deducted. The team with the higher final score wins.
- As a reward, each member of the winning class will earn extra credit, prizes, or whatever reward you and your colleague feel is appropriate.

Chapter Eight

Extra Innings

While you will not find specific games in this chapter, you will find formats to enhance your students' learning through games.

STUDENTS CREATING GAMES (M, H)

Most students enjoy playing games. If you have used games in the classroom, it is probably very clear that they enhance learning and provide the students (and teacher) with an occasion to have some fun. This activity below gives the students the opportunity to create their own games. The objective is to create a game that can be used for learning, reviewing, or practicing skills in the classroom.

- Each student will work in a group of three or four students. You can assign students to groups or allow them to form their own.
- Using classroom time, the students will meet to discuss the type of game they want to create: a game with a sports theme; a board game; a game that models a TV show; or anything else their imaginations can devise.
- Once the game is developed, students will write the procedures to be followed and rules to determine the winner.
- They are to advise you of any materials they need; for example, cardboard, dice, index cards, tape, etc. If the students are unable to supply these materials themselves, do the best you can in getting them.
- After the game rules and procedures have been developed, they are to be turned in to you.
- You then review their work and decide which game(s) are the most appropriate to be used in the classroom. Extra credit or some other reward could

be given to the team(s) that created the best games. (Sometimes just the fact that their game was chosen to be used is reward enough for the students.)
• Then, periodically, the best game(s) can be played throughout the school year for learning concepts or for drill and practice.

HOLIDAY FUN (E, M, H)

Halloween time and the Christmas season are fun times for almost everyone. Most of the games presented in this book can be played at these two exciting times of the year. Instead of using questions based on the subject matter, consider using Halloween and Christmas season trivia questions (or use the subject matter and perhaps have every other question from the list of holiday trivia). Kids seem to enjoy games even more when there is a holiday component to them. Choose the questions you feel are appropriate for your students. For younger students you might consider giving multiple-choice answers.

Halloween Trivia/Legends/Traditions

1. According to legend, this creature can regain human form by putting his clothes back on.
2. The name of this famous vampire means "the son of the devil."
3. The Headless Horseman haunted this colonial New York village.
4. These common symbols of Halloween were first used to ward off evil spirits.
5. Michael Jackson's hit song and video associated with the Halloween season is called _____.
6. According to most superstitions, witches gain their supernatural powers by making a deal with him.
7. Each year the sale of this averages about $2 billion in the United States.
8. This famous entertainer died on Halloween, 1926, after sustaining a blow to his abdomen.
9. According to some folk tales, ghosts and evil spirits can't cross this.
10. According to lore, a witch's life force is stored in this object.
11. Legend holds that this will keep vampires at bay.
12. This word comes from the Saxon word *wicca*, which means "wise one."
13. It was once believed that these creatures protected witches' powers from negative forces.
14. He is said to be the ghost of a soldier killed by a cannon ball during the Revolutionary War.

15. According to superstition, if zombies are fed this it restores their souls and personalities.
16. Tim Burton created this movie after he saw both Halloween and Christmas displays in a store window.
17. In *It's the Great Pumpkin, Charlie Brown*, *he* waits for the Great Pumpkin while the others go out trick or treating.
18. This tradition began when people wore masks to prevent being recognized by ghosts.
19. Carrying jack-o-lanterns is an Irish tradition that started with this vegetable, not pumpkins.
20. Legend has it that if a candle's flame burns blue, one of these is in the house.
21. Lycanthropy is a delusion that a person has turned into this.
22. A TV Guide poll named *Psycho* the second-scariest movie of all time. What was first?
23. In recent years this candy bar has been the most popular treat to hand out on Halloween.
24. This began when families left food on their doorsteps to keep hungry spirits from entering their houses.
25. Legend has it that the ghost of this mobster still haunts Alcatraz Prison.
26. Halloween candy sales account for this percent of the annual sales of the candy industry.
27. _____ and _____ are the Halloween colors: they symbolize harvest and darkness.
28. Some ancient cultures believed these creatures were the ghosts of people who had not yet been reincarnated.
29. Can you afford this costume for Halloween? *Her* dress from MGM's classic movie, *The Wizard of Oz*, sold for $324,188.
30. After he died in 2009, Halloween costume retailers saw the sales of his sequined glove go up 1,000 percent.
31. His character has appeared in over one hundred twenty films.
32. His murders are among the many unsolved cases in crime history. This killer was given nicknames of "The Whitechapel Murderer" and "Leather Apron." He is most commonly known as _____.
33. The nation's largest Halloween celebration, which began about 1923 and is attended by over two million people, is held in this city.
34. Although this movie was first released in 1975, it still plays at midnight every Halloween in New York City.
35. Michael Myers's mask in *Halloween* was actually a modified mask of this 1970s popular TV science fiction series character.
36. In 1682, Bridget Bishop was the first person executed for this.

37. This popular Halloween candy was invented in the 1880's by the Wunderle Candy Company.
38. His character has appeared in close to two hundred films.
39. In some Native American cultures it is believed that these creatures escort the dead to the spirit world.
40. The voice of this famous horror movie actor can be heard in Michael Jackson's *Thriller.*

Answers:

1. Werewolf
2. Dracula
3. Sleepy Hollow
4. Jack-o-lanterns
5. *Thriller*
6. The devil
7. Halloween candy
8. Harry Houdini
9. Running water
10. His/her magic wand
11. Garlic
12. Witch
13. Black cats
14. The Headless Horseman
15. Salt
16. *The Nightmare before Christmas*
17. Linus
18. Dressing up for Halloween
19. Turnips
20. Ghost
21. Werewolf
22. *The Exorcist*
23. Snickers
24. Trick or treating
25. Al Capone
26. 25 percent
27. Orange and black
28. Bats
29. Dorothy
30. Michael Jackson
31. Frankenstein
32. "Jack the Ripper"
33. New York City
34. *The Rocky Horror Picture Show*
35. Captain Kirk
36. Witchcraft
37. Candy corn
38. Count Dracula
39. Owls
40. Vincent Price

Seasonal Trivia

1. More than 1.6 billion of these are made during the holiday season. What are they?
2. What country started the tradition of exchanging gifts?
3. What popular Christmas toy was named after former president Theodore Roosevelt?
4. What is the name of the most famous Christmas ballet?
5. What plant enables you to kiss people at Christmas time?
6. What country is credited with creating eggnog?
7. In *How the Grinch Stole Christmas,* what was the name of the town that the Grinch stole from?
8. In what city did *Miracle on 34th Street* take place?
9. What did the U.S. Postal System first do in 1962?
10. This state, in 1836, became the first one to declare Christmas as a legal holiday.

11. Which of the forty-eight continental states was the last to declare Christmas a legal holiday?

12. What day of the year is considered the busiest shopping day?

13. What character is made of snow and wears a top hat?

14. In the novel *Miracle on 34th Street*, what meat does Kris Kringle refuse to eat?

15. In 2011, Americans bought more than 28 million real ones and almost 12 million fake ones. What are they?

16. Of 365 days a year, what number is Christmas Day?

17. According to superstition, what do oxen do at midnight on Christmas Eve?

18. In 2007, mall Santas in Australia were asked not to say "___, ___, ___" because it was supposedly derogatory to women.

19. This 1946 classic movie appears on TV more often than any other holiday movie. What is it?

20. There are more than five hundred recorded versions, in many languages, of this very popular holiday song. What is it?

21. This red, flowering plant is symbolic of the holiday season. What is it?

22. This story by Charles Dickens, published on December 17, 1843, has been filmed over one hundred times. What is it?

23. Legend has it that King Arthur did this on Christmas Day.

24. Edward Johnson, an assistant to this man, invented Christmas lights in 1882.

25. Over five miles of lights are used to decorate the famous Christmas tree located here.

26. In 1923, he was the first president to light a tree on the White House lawn and introduce the National Christmas Tree Lighting Ceremony.

27. The first picture of the modern-day Santa Claus appeared in an ad by this company.

28. This state harvests more Christmas trees than any other in the United States.

29. It is generally accepted that these were invented to tell the nativity story to those who could not read.

30. This well-known Christmas poem was originally titled "A Visit from St. Nicholas."

31. About 1.5 billion of these are sent each holiday season with the average American family giving and getting about twenty-eight each.

32. What classic Christmas carol is the American version of the German hymn, "O Tannenbaum"?

33. In the song "We Wish You a Merry Christmas," what is it that they want us to bring?

34. In their popular song, what do the Jonas Brothers say they want for Christmas?
35. In *How the Grinch Stole Christmas,* what was the name of the Grinch's dog?
36. In the song "The Twelve Days of Christmas," what are the seven swans doing?
37. In the nativity story, the magi from the East (the three wise men) rode to the manger on what kind of animals?
38. What do female reindeer have that no other female deer have?
39. In what snowy U.S. state is there a town called "North Pole"?
40. What is Mrs. Claus's first name?

Answers:

1. Candy canes
2. Italy (Romans)
3. Teddy bear
4. Nutcracker
5. Mistletoe
6. USA
7. Whoville
8. New York
9. Issued its first Christmas stamps
10. Alabama
11. Oklahoma, in 1907
12. The day after Thanksgiving
13. Frosty the Snowman
14. Venison
15. Christmas trees
16. 359
17. Kneel
18. Ho, Ho, Ho
19. *It's a Wonderful Life*
20. "White Christmas"
21. Poinsettia
22. *A Christmas Carol*
23. Removed the sword from the stone
24. Thomas Edison
25. Rockefeller Center
26. Calvin Coolidge
27. Coca Cola
28. Oregon
29. Christmas carols
30. "The Night Before Christmas"
31. Christmas cards
32. "O Christmas Tree"
33. Figgy pudding
34. A hippopotamus (from the song "All I Want for Christmas Is a Hippopotamus")
35. Max
36. Swimming
37. Camels
38. Antlers
39. Alaska (near Fairbanks)
40. Jessica

Conclusion

As you saw by the results of the survey shown at the beginning of this book, the students who responded feel that games enhance learning and help improve collaborative and study skills. They are also fun and offer a change of pace for you and your students. Consequently, you are encouraged to use them in your classroom in whatever way you see fit to complement your teaching style and to meet the needs of your students.

After you have played a game in class, ask the students for their input. Do this at the end of that class or at the beginning of the next one. Their thoughts on what they derived from the game, the strengths and weaknesses of the game, and any suggestions they have for improvement are sometimes very helpful. Even if the students have no suggestions, they appreciate being asked their opinions.

The objectives of playing games have been explained, the results of a student survey have been analyzed, and a wide variety of games and competitions have been presented for your consideration. Now, *It's Game Time!*

Appendix

CASINO DAY: GAMES ANALYSIS ANSWERS

Two Dice Game—Sums

1. In the space to the right, create a sample space for all possible *sums* when rolling two dice. *See below.*
2. What is the probability of rolling an odd sum? *18/36 or 1/2*
3. What is the probability of rolling an even sum? *18/36 or 1/2*
4. Is this a fair game? *Yes.* Why? *Each player has an equal chance of winning.*

	1	*2*	*3*	*4*	*5*	*6*
1	2	3	4	5	6	7
2	3	4	5	6	7	8
3	4	5	6	7	8	9
4	5	6	7	8	9	10
5	6	7	8	9	10	11
6	7	8	9	10	11	12

Two Dice Game—Products

1. In the space to the right, create a sample space for all possible *products* when rolling two dice. *See below.*
2. What is the probability of rolling an odd product? *9/36 or 1/4*
3. What is the probability of rolling an even product? *27/36 or 3/4*
4. Is this a fair game? *No.* Why? *Each player does not have an equal chance of winning.*

	1	2	3	4	5	6
1	1	2	3	4	5	6
2	2	4	6	8	10	12
3	3	6	9	12	15	18
4	4	8	12	16	20	24
5	5	10	15	20	25	30
6	6	12	18	24	30	36

Chips Ahoy

1. Make a sample space of the possible outcomes. *See below. For the purpose of the analysis, we will assume we are using two red chips and two white chips.* Hint: Think of the chips as Rl, R2, Wl, W2.
2. What is the probability of Rl R2? *1/6 (note that R2 Rl is the same outcome)*?
3. What is the probability of W1 W2? *1/6*
4. What is the probability of drawing two chips of the same color? *2/6 = 1/3*
5. Is this a fair game? *No.* Why? *The probability of the player winning is 1/3 while the probability of the house winning is 2/3. For the game to be fair, the house should pay off $2, not $1, each time the player wins.*

Sample Space: R1 R2, R1 W1, R1 W2, R2 W1, R2 W2, W1 W2

The Great Race

1. How many possible outcomes are there? *Six*
2. What is the probability of racer #1 winning? *1/6*
3. What is the probability of racer #2 winning? *1/6*
4. What is the probability of racer #3 winning? *1/6*
5. What is the probability of racer #4 winning? *1/6*
6. What is the probability of racer #5 winning? *1/6*
7. What is the probability of racer #6 winning? *1/6*
8. Assuming all six racers were bet on, how much does the House initially collect? *$6.* After paying off the winner, has the House won or lost? *Won.* How much? *$2*
9. Does every racer have an equal chance of winning? *Yes*
10. If you consider player against player only, is this a fair game? *Yes.* Why? *Each player has an equal chance of winning.*
11. In this game, can the House lose? *No.* Explain. *The House always wins $2 if all the racers are bet on.*

Random Faces

1. How many possible outcomes are there? (Hint: suit doesn't matter.) *13 (A, 2, 3, 4, 5, 6, 7, 8, 9, 10, J, Q, K)*
2. What is the probability of drawing a Jack, Queen, or King? *3/13*
3. If you play this game thirteen times, how many times should you expect to win? *3*
4. After having played the game thirteen times, you should expect to have (choose one) won/lost $1. *(Win $9, lose $10)*
5. Considering that you are playing against the House, is this a fair game? *No.* Why? *The House has a better chance of winning.*

After analyzing the five games played on Casino Day, what conclusion(s) have you come to? *Answers will vary.*

Some possible responses: not all games are fair; the House has a better chance of winning than the players; when you gamble you usually lose.

Suggested Race Track for Casino Day

Place each racer in the Starting Gate.

Starting Gate   Finish Line

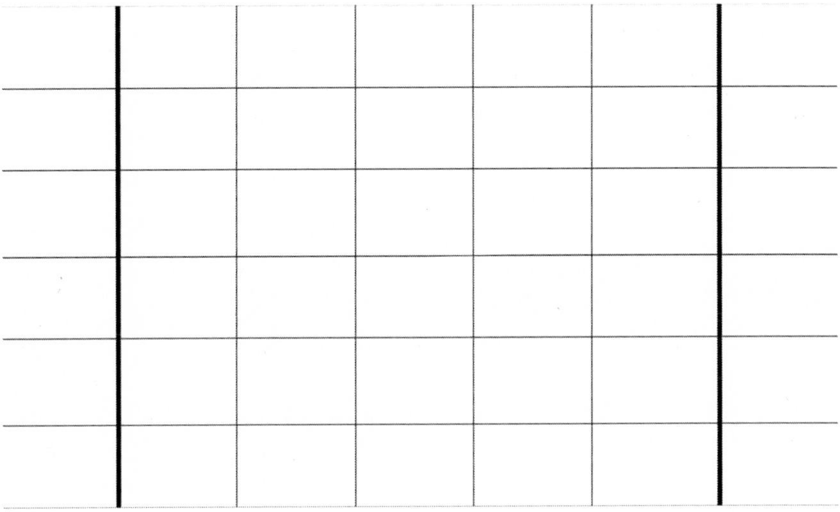

Figure D01.1

Casino Day Play Money

For durability, run off on heavy duty paper such as oak tag. Also consider personalizing the money by including your school's name, motto, logo, etc.

$ 1	$ 1
$ 1	$ 1
$ 1	$ 1
$ 1	$ 1
$ 1	$ 1

Figure D01.2

SAMPLE ENGLISH JEOPARDY BOARD

Point Value	Name the Part of Speech (word in italics)	Word Changes	Grab Bag
10	Jessica owns a *red* car.	Give the contraction for "he would."	Which of the following is a synonym for "home"? Cellar, interior, residence
20	Justin *ran* home.	Spell the plural of "hero."	A limerick has this many lines.
30	Stephanie was *very* happy!	Change the word "like" into a word which means "not liked."	*Ice* is to *water* as *solid* is to _____.
40	Brianna made a pot *of* soup.	Add a suffix to "sleep" to form a word that means "ready for sleep."	State the comparative form of "grateful."
50	*He* loves pizza.	Make two words by rearranging the letters in the word "polo."	Which does not belong? Dictionary, atlas, almanac, novel, encyclopedia

Figure D01.3

Answers

Parts of Speech: (10) adjective (20) verb (30) adverb (40) preposition (50) pronoun

Word Changes: (10) he'd (20) heroes (30) disliked (40) sleepy (50) pool, loop

Grab Bag: (10) residence (20) five (30) liquid (40) more grateful (50) novel (not used for reference)

SAMPLE MATH JEOPARDY BOARD

Point Value	Number Please	Measurements	Tricky Math
10	The average of 62, 42, and 25	# of centimeters in a meter	divide 30 by 1/2 and add 10
20	Largest prime number less than 40	Number of square feet in a square yard	half a half dozen
30	The quotient of 595 and 17	Number of feet in a mile	Number of minutes from two to two until two two
40	Number in a baker's dozen	Number of pints in a gallon	25 divided by 0
50	# of letters in the name of the longest river in the USA	# of cubic inches in a cubic foot	# of haystacks if 2 1/4 haystacks are added to to 3 1/2 haystacks

Figure D01.4

Answers

Number Please: (10) 43 (20) 37 (30) 35 (40) 13 (50) 11
Measurements: (10) 100 (20) 9 (30) 5280 (40) 8 (50) 1728
Tricky Math: (10) 70 (20) 3 (30) 4 (40) division by zero is undefined (50) one

SAMPLE SCIENCE JEOPARDY BOARD

Point Value	Our Solar System	Planet Earth	Grab Bag
10	It is the third planet from the sun.	Is the careful use of our planet's resources called condensation, preservation, or conservation?	A chair will not move unless somebody moves it. Is this an example of impetus, momentum, or inertia?
20	This planet has rings.	Is the continent of Antarctica best described as a prairie, a desert or a tundra?	This is a large hairy fruit that bears the seeds of a palm tree.
30	This is the largest planet.	What is the name given to the region of the earth between the core and the crust?	This is the saltiest body of water on earth; it is 9 times saltier than the oceans.
40	This planet is closest in size to Earth.	What large ocean current carries a stream of warm water from the Gulf of Mexico toward Europe?	In computer technology, the letters "CPU" are an abbreviation for what?
50	The asteroid belt is located between these two planets.	This gas makes up about 78% of the earth's atmosphere.	This famous scientist once said, "Invention is 10% inspiration and 90% perspiration."

Figure D01.5

Answers

Solar System: (10) Earth (20) Saturn (30) Jupiter (40) Venus (50) Mars and Jupiter

Planet Earth: (10) conservation (20) desert (30) the mantle (40) the Gulf Stream (50) nitrogen

Grab Bag: (10) inertia (20) coconut (30) the Dead Sea (40) central processing unit (50) Thomas Edison

SAMPLE SOCIAL STUDIES JEOPARDY BOARD

Point Value	The Civil War	The 20th Century	Grab Bag
10	Which became the most important crop in the southern states? Tobacco, cotton, wheat.	What "crashed" in 1929 ending an economic boom in America?	The system of _____ & _____ limits the power of government branches.
20	What was the name of the army that fought for the North?	This city is the headquarters of the United Nations.	America's birthday is on this date: month, day, & year
30	Who shot President Lincoln in 1865?	This inspirational landmark greeted early immigrants as they sailed into New York harbor.	In the military, what does it mean when a soldier is "AWOL"?
40	He is quoted as saying, "A house divided against itself cannot stand."	When Ronald Reagan was President, who was Vice President?	The most serious crime an American citizen can commit against the government is this.
50	This Civil War hero became the 18th president in 1868.	What were the last 2 states to become part of the USA in 1959?	Which two Johnsons became President when the president in office was assassinated?

Figure D01.6

Answers

Civil War: (10) cotton (20) the Union Army (30) John Wilkes Booth (40) Abraham Lincoln (50) Ulysses S. Grant

The 20th Century: (10) Wall St. stock market (20) New York (30) The Statue of Liberty (40) George W. Bush (50) Hawaii and Alaska

Grab Bag: (10) checks and balances (20) July 4, 1776 (30) absent without leave (40) treason (50) Andrew Johnson (after Lincoln) and Lyndon Johnson (after Kennedy)

SAMPLE TEAM TOURNAMENT SCORE CARD

Student Name	Team Name	Tally	Pts. Earned	Tournament Pts.
Babe R.	A	~~HHH~~ I	6	5
Lou G.	B	III	3	2
Joe D.	C	~~HHH~~	5	4
Mickey M.	D	~~HHH~~ IIII	9	6
Reggie J.	E	II	2	1
Derek J.	F	~~HHH~~	5	4

Figure D01.7

Above is a score card from *one* of perhaps three or four large groups of students.

	Team A	Team B	Team C	Team D	Team E	Team F
	Babe 5	Lou 2	Joe 4	Mickey 6	Reggie 1	Derek 4
	2	1	5	1	5	2
	3	6	4	2	4	3
	1		5	3		1
Totals:	**11**	**9**	**18**	**12**	**10**	**10**

Scores that do not have names next to them represent students in other groups and on other score cards. Dividing the above totals by 4, 3, 4, 4, 3, and 4 respectively (the number of members of each team) results in the final team scores of 2.75, 3.0, 4.5, 3.0, 3.3, and 2.5.

Final results:

First place: Team C

Second place: Team E

Third Place: tie Team B and Team D

TEAM TOURNAMENT SCORE CARDS

Student Name	Team Name	Tally	Pts. Earned	Tournament Pts.

Figure D01.8

TEAM TOURNAMENT CHALLENGE SHEET

Name _____   Team _____

Question # ___ My challenge answer is _____

Question # ___ My challenge answer is _____

Question # ___ My challenge answer is _____

Question # ___ My challenge answer is _____

Question # ___ My challenge answer is _____

Question # ___ My challenge answer is _____

Question # ___ My challenge answer is _____

Question # ___ My challenge answer is _____

Question # ___ My challenge answer is _____

Question # ___ My challenge answer is _____

Question # ___ My challenge answer is _____

Question # ___ My challenge answer is _____

Question # ___ My challenge answer is _____

Question # ___ My challenge answer is _____

Question # ___ My challenge answer is _____

Question # ___ My challenge answer is _____

Question # ___ My challenge answer is _____

Question # ___ My challenge answer is _____

Question # ___ My challenge answer is _____

Question # ___ My challenge answer is _____

Question # ___ My challenge answer is _____

Question # ___ My challenge answer is _____

Question # ___ My challenge answer is _____

Question # ___ My challenge answer is _____

Question # ___ My challenge answer is _____

Question # ___ My challenge answer is _____

Question # ___ My challenge answer is _____

Question # ___ My challenge answer is _____

Question # ___ My challenge answer is _____

Question # ___ My challenge answer is _____

1	2	3	4	5	6	7
8	9	10	11	12	13	14
15	16	17	18	19	20	21
22	23	24	25	26	27	28
29	30	31	32	33	34	35
36	37	38	39	40	41	42
43	44	45	46	47	48	49
50	51	52	53	54	55	56
57	58	59	60	TRIPLE POINT VALUE	DOUBLE POINT VALUE	DOUBLE POINT VALUE

Figure D01.9

This is the number array for the Team Tournament.

1	1	1	1	1
2	2	2	2	2
3	3	3	3	4
4	4	4	5	5
5	5	6	6	6

Figure D01.10

For Twenty-One in Chapter 7